MANAGE YOUR EXPECTATIONS

Let the Numbers Do the Talking

JACQUELINE EDDY
with consulting attorney **MARSHALL KARRO**

Scripture quotations are taken from The Holy Bible, New International
Version®, NIV® Copyright © 1973, 1978, 1984, 2011 by Biblica,
Inc.® Used by permission. All rights reserved worldwide.

Archway Publishing books may be ordered through booksellers or by contacting:

Archway Publishing
1663 Liberty Drive
Bloomington, IN 47403
www.archwaypublishing.com
1 (888) 242-5904

ISBN: 978-1-4808-7418-3 (sc)
ISBN: 978-1-4808-7417-6 (e)

Library of Congress Control Number: 2019900800

Print information available on the last page.

Archway Publishing rev. date: 02/08/2019

ACKNOWLEDGEMENTS

This book represents an effort to bring comfort, peace, practicality, reality and efficiency to the divorce process. While there has been much chatter in the industry about the concept of **The Collaborative Law Divorce Process**, an effort that advocates an interest-based approach to mediation, there is still so much adversity and animosity. It is my hope that this publication will further promote the awareness and benefits of **The Collaborative Law Divorce Process**.

I have a great desire to help make the divorce process efficient and manageable. Personal experience and connection with others prompted me to create this guide to make this significant life transition easier, more cost effective and, most importantly, empowering to all who find themselves in this difficult situation.

It was a pleasure and an honor to be able to work with Marshall Karro as a consulting attorney for this guide. Marshall stated that his incentive to be a part of the publication of this guide was the fact that after years of experience in the courtroom, he had struggled with the unnecessary chaos of the adversarial approach to divorce and the resulting toxicity and detriment of the parties who, in many cases, were also parents of children. He feels strongly that many cases can be settled with agreements that are secured through a process, which is solution oriented as opposed to winning by any means within the judicial rulebook. This book could not have been created or published without his expertise.

At my first Certified Divorce Financial Analyst conference I had the pleasure of meeting Douglas I. Donald, MBA, CPA/PFS, CRPC, Cr.FA, CDFA who so graciously provided a peer review of this publication. Donald is one of the most generous and considerate professionals that I have ever had the pleasure of working with and I value his opinions and input.

I would especially like to thank the following people who were instrumental in my personal divorce recovery: Carolina Checa, Gladys Espinel, Kari Gras, Melissa Harding, Peggy Herbert, Michelle Kasak, Sharon and Donny Lainhart, Anne Paramour, Kathy Sawrey, Linda Soldo, Tammy Ward and my wonderful family whose love and support have grounded me. I would also like to thank Sheila and John Fassler who gave me a job after my own divorce and the entrepreneurial inspiration to pursue this endeavor and my wonderful husband who helped me to the finish line!

But most importantly, I would like to thank God for being my sunshine, my courage and my strength! By allowing myself to trust in God, I was able to find my way!

Table of Contents

A divorce guide designed to empower you

Reference Documents

FOREWORD

I believe in marriage. Everyone who gets married assumes it will be forever. It isn't always, and the expectation does not have the power to ruin your life. I fear I am part of a dying breed that still believes that love conquers all. Research states that more than 60% of marriages end in divorce today. Albeit a staggering amount, even more second marriages fail. So you must be reading this book because you are facing divorce. I'm sorry your marriage didn't work out. However, this book can help you gain some knowledge to have a successful and collaborative experience.

The author, Jacqueline Eddy, has done her homework both personally and professionally in the writing of this book. Within the following pages, you will discover skills and tools you can use. Try to make this divorce process into a possibly positive experience for you and your spouse.

The context of this book will assist you to lessen your stress and anxiety as you plan your divorce, interact with loved ones and professionals, and negotiate a settlement you can both live with for the near future. Most individuals don't want to go to war. They want to move on with their dignity intact. If you choose to be adversarial, I'm sure hostility will boomerang back to you. However, if the choices reflect a sense of moving through the process as fairly as you can, the rewards will be numerous.

So is it possible to have a collaborative and successful divorce? Yes, it is possible. It isn't going to be easy, but if both individuals face the process with maturity, mutual goals, and stay on track, i.e. focused, it is possible.

Again my sorrow that you are reading these pages and finding yourself on the road to divorce. The journey can be long, tedious and expensive; or it can be civil, collaborative and kind. The choice, as there will be many of those in your future, is completely up to you. Just remember that the suffering ends; the grief lessens. Joy and happiness will fill your heart again.

Be well.

INTRODUCTION

Empowering you

"Nearly all men can stand adversity, but if you want to test a man's character, give him power."

- Abraham Lincoln

Isn't this what divorce comes down to? A power struggle over who will win, get things, come out better than the other, keep the kids or the dogs! In the end, do you really win? This guide is not intended as a promotion of divorce, but addresses the fact that divorce is sometimes inevitable. Nearly 50% of all marriages end in divorce, and the percentages are significantly higher for second and third marriages. In my opinion, a substantial part of this increase is due to the enactment of the no-fault divorce laws and the fact that getting divorced is sadly becoming more culturally accepted. The process of divorce is even more daunting because the courts are backlogged, there is an inability to compromise and the time it takes to complete the divorce process has become a burden on each party and their families.

I have had a variety of experiences from working in public accounting with Ernst & Young and PricewaterhouseCoopers LLP to chairing committees in my local schools and township to serving on the board of directors for a non-profit organization. But none of these experiences prepared me for the emotional and financial devastation of divorce. I ended up mediating my divorce settlement but came away with intense thoughts that "_There has to be a better way._" I began coaching individuals through referrals from my church, and after much research began to learn more about **The Collaborative Law Divorce Process**. A crucial component of this process is an evaluation of the parties' financial situation through an analysis by a CDFA/CPA, which basically "_lets the numbers do the talking._" Analytically, this sparked my interest and further emphasized the fact that so many of the decisions to be made in the divorce process are based on the financial position of the parties. By preparing financial scenarios, each party can make better and more personal decisions. This information is not only extremely valuable to the individuals but also to the attorneys and mediators. The reality of the legal parameters and the numbers help address and manage client expectations.

I have had the distinct honor and blessing of working with Marshall Karro, a practicing divorce lawyer in Charlotte, North Carolina in consultation while writing this reference guide. He has been in practice since 1973 and is a leader in the field of divorce mediation and collaborative divorce. He is a certified Family Financial Mediator and a certified Superior Court Mediator who has mediated more than 3,000 family conflict cases since 1995. He is an equally passionate advocate of the non-adversarial collaborative law process. Marshall is also a certified Level One Collaborative Divorce attorney and a founding member of the Charlotte Collaborative Divorce Professionals, a select group of attorneys, financial neutrals, divorce coaches and child specialists dedicated to the efficiency and values of collaborative law approach to conflict resolution.

Marshall has served as wonderful mentor, advocate and invaluable resource. His insights and genuine humanity towards couples, especially those with children, has been instrumental in gathering information that would directly benefit those struggling through the divorce process.

So where do you begin?

If your intention is to save money, make the most of the assets you have and separate as amicably as possible, we suggest **The Collaborative Law Divorce Process**. This process begins by having <u>the singular goal of creating a complete and thorough agreement that specifically addresses the needs of each party given his/her financial situation</u>. This approach is in direct contrast to the traditional adversarial methods used in the divorce process whereby each party is represented by his/her attorney and the purpose is to get as much as you can from the process or to give as little as you can. There is a tremendous amount of wasted efforts on emotional expectations and duplication of costs to produce financial information to ensure full disclosure. **The Collaborative Law Divorce Process** bridges this gap by providing an interest-based negotiation model for resolving disputes. This process provides each party with legal representation and makes use of a financial neutral, a Certified Divorce Financial Analyst (CDFA), to prepare scenarios for consideration to make the most equitable distribution in the best interests of **EACH** party and their family members. Most individuals do not realize that all assets are not created equal and that there are a multitude of special circumstances and tax implications that affect the distribution and ultimate value of a given asset. *See Appendix A for a case scenario*. While this case may appear to be an overly simplistic "recipe" for divorce, each collaborative professional is aware that this is an extremely emotional event and probably the most significant personal financial transaction in which each party will ever be engaged. The collaborative law attorneys have obtained additional training to receive this designation, and their purpose is to act equitably to promote resolution—not controversy.

<u>Negotiating in this manner provides numerous benefits, including but not limited to the following</u>:

- Assures each party has personal legal representation (as opposed to other forms of mediation)
- Addresses the expectations of each party based on his/her financial circumstances
- Reduces the amount of emotional stress and time wasted when the focus is on the outcome and not the past
- Avoids duplicate costs when parties are upfront and share information
- Obtains an agreement in a timely manner so each party can move forward with his/her life
- Lessens drama when issues are addressed based on the familial needs and overall available resources of the case

Many clients and individuals engaging in the divorce process have unrealistic expectations and usually **WASTE** a great deal of time and money. In a majority of cases, there is only so much money to be allocated, so we strongly advise you to make the most of those assets for the benefit of each party and your families. The sayings, "I will take him for everything he's got" or "I will quit my job so she doesn't get anything" in most cases are simply not true. It doesn't mean that this process will not be difficult because it will. Your family is being separated, and each party will have to make serious adjustments to his/her lifestyles and adapt to this new scenario.

Whether you like it or not, if there are children involved, you will be enmeshed in each other's lives for many years, and the decisions made during the divorce process will have a *long-term impact* on each party involved.

This is an investment in yourself and your future.
You owe it to yourself to pursue an option that ensures that you will have a concise and complete divorce agreement that takes into account your personal needs as well as incorporating proper legal guidance.

Focusing on resolution provides immediate *cost benefits* and having legal advice through individual representation gives each party confidence that all areas are being addressed within the parameters and guidelines of the law.

This guide has been prepared to give you a general overview of the divorce process and to increase your awareness of what to expect and items to consider based on your personal situation. We hope you will find this guide to be a good reference or resource to ensure that you are addressing applicable areas in a logical and definitive manner.

All opinions and presentation of material has been gathered and outlined by myself. Marshall has provided the sample legal clauses and has given guidance on items that should be considered, and I have provided items to consider based on the financial impacts of each clause presented. I want to emphasize that the material presented is not to be interpreted as legal or financial advice but an outline of the divorce process and things you may encounter that may apply to your particular situation. <u>Please use the material presented for your reference and consult with your attorney/CDFA.</u>

Our goal is to make this significant life transition easier, more cost effective and, most importantly, <u>Empower You</u> to make the best decisions possible for a brighter future.

Part I of this book provides information to help you understand your situation and determine what will be the most manageable and cost-effective approach for your individual situation.

Part II provides information on the areas that are typically addressed in a divorce agreement along with personal priorities, items to consider, examples from executed agreements and room to take notes as you consider each area. This section is broken down into four areas: *agreements related to children, agreements related to marital* *assets, agreements related to spousal support and other pertinent agreements* that may be applicable.

Part III encourages you to embrace your future and provides direction and resources that will help you move on with *Dignity* and *Grace.*

So, get out your highlighter and mark everything that applies to you.

We have included documents and additional resources in the appendices that may be helpful as well. We encourage you to share your concerns with your attorney and/or mediator. Whether you are contemplating a divorce or are amidst a divorce, an analysis of your financial situation will be the guide to nearly all your decisions and the final outcome of your divorce. *Let the numbers do the talking,* and take the time to review options that would be most beneficial.

PART I
Determining what is best for your situation

CHAPTER 1
Evaluating Your Situation

"Strong feelings do not necessarily make a strong character. The strength of a man is to be measured by the power of the feelings he subdues not by the power of those which subdue him."

-William Carleton

You've decided you want a divorce or your spouse has asked for a divorce. You are now in panic mode and are either scared to death, emotionally devastated or extremely angry. While things may appear overwhelming, be patient with yourself. Do not beat your self up or fall into the deep, dark negative abyss of the blame game. This is a time when you will need to allow yourself to vent and grieve, but it is also a time to plan and protect yourself. As many counselors will advise, divorce is more about a death of your dreams rather than about the failure of the marriage or losing your partner. Each and every one of us deserves to be treated kindly and have the unconditional love and support of our partners. This concept will be addressed in more detail in Chapter 7, which focuses on moving forward. Though you may have been mistreated in some way, it is imperative to try to stay in the moment and forget the past for right now. By doing this, you mindfully position yourself at the helm of your future. As a result, you will be able to honestly assess your personal situation so you (and nobody else) can decide what is best for you.

**Divorce by nature is adversarial, but the
divorce process does not have to be.**

Whether you think your divorce will be amicable or not, there is a reason why you no longer want to be together. There is bound to be controversy when trying to reach an agreement to separate. Each party will have his/her perceived desired outcome of the divorce process, and this contrived outcome will be distorted further by the influence of family, friends and new partners. This is why it is *important* to have *legal and financial professionals* involved to legally protect your interests, promote resolution, manage your expectations and determine financial implications.

**Let's review the various options, and you
can determine what is best for you.**

Since 95% of all divorce cases are settled out of court, the focus of this chapter is on the alternative methods to settle divorce disputes: Non-Attorney Mediators, Attorney Mediators, and **The Collaborative Law Divorce Process.** Each of these methods allows each party to have more control over the process and its final outcome. Some additional benefits of settling divorce through these methods include the following:

- It is typically a more cost-effective approach.
- Details of your agreement will not be on public record (optional).
- You will have the final decisive authority on clauses in your agreement rather than accepting decisions of a judge or third party.

While on the surface, these options may appear to be the best approach personally and financially, that is not always the case. Your attorney will be able to advise you and protect your interests.

Working with a Non-Attorney Mediator:

- The parties feel they can negotiate a settlement on their own behalf.
- The parties want to save money.
- The mediator ensures that he/she will review all significant areas of a divorce agreement but cannot offer legal advice or financial counsel.
- The mediator will prepare a Memorandum of Understanding, which is basically a draft of your agreement, and an attorney (usually an associate of the mediator) will be engaged to prepare the final legally binding agreement.
- The parties usually negotiate on their own behalf and consult with attorneys separately if they choose to do so.

Beware:

While there are many reputable non-attorney mediators, we encourage you to take the time to assess their reputation. Before you engage their services, they will require you to sign an agreement that has a disclaimer that protects them from litigation.

Example clause in a non-attorney mediator agreement:
The parties agree that neither will call the consultant to testify concerning any consultation or any statements or admissions made during the course of consultation which are not otherwise discoverable through the legal process, including, but not limited to, notes, records, written and oral communications, draft options, and work product of the consultant. In the event that either party contravenes this position, the consultant will move to quash the subpoena or summons, and the party in breach shall pay all of the consultant's fees and expenses for so doing.

In addition, they may terminate their agreement with you if things become too controversial or difficult, while retaining the initial fee.

Example clause in a non-attorney mediator agreement:
The party or parties acknowledge that either party has the right to terminate the consultation before an agreement is reached.

Additionally, <u>the consultants may terminate mediation under the following circumstances</u>:

(a) The failure of a party or parties to provide honest and accurate answers or information regarding assets, liabilities, income, and expenses;
(b) The consultant's belief that further consultation sessions would not be productive or worth the time and expense;
(c) <u>Any reason deemed appropriate by the consultant.</u>

There are a great deal of practicing non-attorney mediators that will sell you on the benefits of mediation, and while all of these assertions in theory may be true, you will be charged a fee for their mediation services, another fee if you try to consult with an attorney on the side and yet another fee for an attorney to make your agreement legal and binding. These are additional and sometimes substantial costs. <u>There is also a significant potential for miscommunication without a cohesive network of parties, so be sure to reread your final document to ensure there are no changes and that you understand all the clauses that have been included. A financial review of your agreement is highly recommended during the course of your negotiations and, at the very least, prior to your signing the final agreement.</u>

It is customary for all mediators (non-attorney as well as attorney mediators) to encourage each party to have separate legal representation. Although, many attorneys are reluctant to just consult or review an agreement because they are not privy to all the information gathered and are asked to give an opinion on an agreement without proper background information. As a result, there are many details that can be overlooked, and the couple may experience a great deal of stress because of these omissions or vague language. While we realize that this may appear to be a more cost-effective approach, in many cases it can be very detrimental.

The decisions you are making during the divorce process affect you and your children for many years to come. There have been numerous cases where the results have been more stressful and costly due to inexperience, lack of knowledge and financial acumen, ambiguous language and false assurances.

Working with an Attorney Mediator:

- The parties feel it can negotiate a settlement on their own behalf.
- The parties want to save money.
- The parties feel they have enough information to make decisions and want an attorney mediator who can help negotiate with knowledge of the legal statutes.
- The parties feel that an attorney mediator will have more experience with and information related to final settlements within the court system as well as ones settled outside the courts.
- The parties may choose to have individual representation during the negotiation process.

The difference with attorney mediators is that they can provide valuable suggestions based on their experience and knowledge of your state's family law statutes and can provide a more complete Memorandum of Understanding. While the attorney mediator is not legally representing either party, it is comforting to note that attorneys are held ethically accountable because the issuance and maintenance of their licenses are regulated by the applicable state bar associations. During mediation, they are essentially only facilitating the process while providing legal explanations or suggestions to both parties. Legal explanations do not suffice for legal guidance. By definition, a mediator is a third party that is engaged to aid in conflict resolution but not to advise or make decisions for the parties involved. This is why attorney mediators may also suggest or recommend that each party obtain independent personal representation. While having separate representation is advised, there is still duplication of costs, and the intent is to get the best settlement for each individual—not necessarily the individuals in aggregate or the family unit.

Emergence of The Collaborative Law Divorce Process:

While divorce negotiations follow family law statutes, these statutes cannot address all the needs of family situations, and the outcome is left up to a judge. Divorce contracts are/were becoming a means of revenge or punishment, and the best (highest paid negotiator/attorney) would win.

This distrust of the legal profession and inefficiency of providing a fair contract was the inspiration behind the philosophy of **The Collaborative Law Divorce Process.** Many attorneys felt that they were unable to properly serve the best interest of their clients and/or divorcing couples efficiently and proceeded to create a different approach. Each marriage is unique, and the parties involved have a variety of members as well as varying personal and emotional interests. The family law statutes themselves cannot address the multitude of diverse situations and, therefore, more people are seeking alternative forms of conflict resolution.

Let's consider some other legally negotiated contracts where attorneys lead the process:

- Would you purchase a car without having a warranty or assurances that protect your rights that the vehicle you are purchasing is in good working order and there is certain recourse if things are not handled properly before you sign a purchase agreement?
- Would you purchase a home/property without an inspection or a proper legal document that provides recourse and assurances that you have clear title, the property is free of hazardous waste or materials, the property has the proper zoning for its intended use and everything is in good working order?

The difference in negotiating a divorce contract compared to the situations described above is that the majority of people have trust and confidence in the attorneys who prepared the documents to close on their home or the sales agreement to purchase a car. How many of you can honestly say that you have read your entire home purchase agreement or sales contract when purchasing a car or a home? You inherently trusted that the documents were complete and protected your interests based on consumer protection laws.

There has been and is a deep resentment around the unfairness of the divorce process and those who facilitate the continued controversy. More and more individuals are not only looking to save money in the divorce process, but also feel that it can be achieved better with as little assistance or involvement of attorneys as possible.

The Collaborative Law Divorce Process:

- Each party has concerns and interests and wants to be heard.
- The parties want to participate in a process that promotes resolution and is cost effective.
- The parties want to make the most of their assets and have confidence that a fair and equitable agreement will be reached.
- The collaborative law attorneys have engaged in additional training to receive this designation and are bound to provide resolution in or out of the court setting.
- The parties and their attorneys are willing to share information and provide full disclosure of the assets and necessary information.
- A financial neutral is involved to provide options to consider that take into account the personal needs of each party and the resources available.

- Each party wants legal representation to negotiate on its behalf.
- Each party signs a collaborative agreement that states that the parties will try to reach an agreement, but if they are unable to do so will have to find other representation if they choose to go to court. ***See Appendix B for a copy of a Collaborative Divorce Engagement Agreement.***

The Collaborative Law Divorce Process is bringing back confidence in the family law legal process and their professionals by demonstrating that they in fact have a genuine interest in the outcome and welfare of their clients and their families. By focusing on resolution, providing legal guidance and incorporating the services of a financial neutral (CDFA to provide financial options), the parties will be able to create a more complete agreement in an efficient and cost-effective manner.

This is an investment in your future.
Make the most of this opportunity.

The idea of holding out as long as you can to get what you want or bombarding your partner with unnecessary requests only hurts everyone involved, drags out the process and increases the cost for both parties.

In summary, The Collaborative Law Divorce Process includes the following:

An attorney for each party that will:
- Advise you of the laws in your state
- Advise you of the fees involved
- Listen to your interests and represent them
- Be respectful, honest and advocate for your interests
- Speak on your behalf and manage emotional situations
- Negotiate on your behalf and engage services of a CDFA (the financial neutral) to provide financial options (usually a shared expense)

- Work directly with the other party's attorney to gather all necessary documentation
- Clarify any unusual language and point out unreasonable expectations
- <u>Not go to court if you do not reach an agreement – a collaborative agreement between the client and their attorney states that the attorney is engaged to provide an out of court settlement.</u> ***See Appendix B***

In practice, the couples get together with their attorneys and discuss the process and review options provided by the CDFA to obtain an equitable agreement, given the legal statutes and financial circumstances. Each attorney will guide his/her client through the process, manage expectations and help the client ascertain what is reasonable and most cost beneficial to each party based on the financial information provided. Sometimes the cost of getting what you want will far exceed the benefit. If emotions are high, there are ways to manage the negotiation process, and it is proactive to have resolution-based attorneys to manage these difficult situations.

> *Let the numbers do the talking and let the attorneys inform and give advice based on experience and the laws specific to your state or jurisdiction.*

A CDFA (financial neutral) that will, depending on your financial situation:

- Work independently to identify your financial situation
- Prepare written proposals for alimony, child support and distribution of assets
- Prepare tax calculations for each individual, asset allocations and applicable exemptions
- Assist with the preparation of a qualified domestic relations order (QDRO) used for the separation of retirement assets
- Assist with budgeting and future financial projections

While **The Collaborative Law Divorce Process** emphasizes the use of a financial-neutral individual (CDFA), it is important to understand that this individual should be professional and knowledgeable. Costs of these professionals may vary but so will your needs based on the amount of assets to be separated and difficulty of your financial situation. I highly recommend the use of a CDFA, which is a fairly new designation, and one who uses some type of divorce family law software to efficiently prepare an overview of your financial situation and items to consider based on your specific situation.

A Divorce Coach (optional) that will:
- Provide emotional coaching during and after the divorce process
- Provide tools to focus on positive outcomes
- Provide resources and assistance in planning your future
- Help you transition to your new life

Even in the most difficult situations, **The Collaborative Law Divorce Process** has been successful because it offers a non-adversarial approach while providing legal representation and a systematic process to save money, reduce tension, lessen anxiety and provide an outcome that addresses the present as well as future interests of each party. While we understand that there may be situations where the legal system must be used, we still recommend you review the sections of this book that may relate to your case and formulate priorities that will be best suited for your personal situation.

The Collaborative Law Divorce Process embraces an approach to help families move on in a more amicable manner and with the intention of benefiting the whole family. We encourage you to review *Appendix A* for a case scenario. This case scenario was prepared to show a simple example based on real clients and how the collaborative process can provide benefits to both parties. The presentation of information allows each party to quickly and efficiently review his/her financial situation based on personal interests and circumstances. While this case is somewhat simplistic, you can imagine the _increased cost savings_ when there are larger amounts of assets and more complicated personal circumstances. In the end, nearly all decisions are based on the numbers: the value of marital assets and the amount of available income.

Listed below are some additional questions that you should ask yourself and that will help you assess your situation and the professionals assisting you throughout the divorce process.

Questions to help you assess your situation:

1. Are you familiar with and aware of your marital finances?
2. Do you have access to all checking, savings and investment accounts?
3. Do you have a complete understanding of your retirement savings, pension and other company benefits provided to you and/or your spouse?
4. Can you prepare a budget for yourself?
5. Can you prepare a budget for your children's expenses?
6. Can you prepare a list of your assets and those of your spouse?
7. Do you have confidence that your spouse will share all financial and benefit information?

If you answered NO to any of the above questions, we highly recommend that you consult with an attorney and a CDFA to gain a better understanding of how you can assess your financial situation and future options. Even if you can answer YES to all of the above, it would still be prudent to consult with an attorney and a CDFA to review financial options and strategies based on your personal situation, tax laws and distribution options.

Other more specific questions include:

1. Do you or your spouse own your own business?
2. Is your spouse reluctant to share financial information with you?

3. Has your spouse spent significant amounts of money or increased your credit card debt?
4. Do you have reason to believe your spouse is/was dishonest?
5. Is there a new partner in your life or that of your spouse?

If you answered YES to any of the above questions, it would be most prudent for you to engage the services of an attorney and a CDFA. This would ensure all assets are accounted for, accurate and reasonable valuations will be obtained and financial evidence can be provided in a timely manner.

Based on your circumstance, you will have a choice to be vindictive, antagonistic, taken advantage of or true to yourself. You are truly successful when you can look at the decisions you made and feel secure in the fact that "given the information at the time, I was adequately informed and acted with grace and integrity." We are here to help you to accomplish that! Put the past behind you and focus on the future.

Let the numbers do the talking, and with proper planning, you will have clarity.

Summary:

The divorce process has legal parameters or guidelines by state that establish precedents, but, in truth, divorce is about negotiation. During a time when you are emotionally stressed, you may not be in the best state of mind to make decisions that will or may affect your future and that of your children. This is why many couples immediately hire a lawyer. Hopefully from the information presented above, you will consider and research **Collaborative Law Attorneys first**. These attorneys will be best suited to evaluate your situation and determine/advise you of the best approach based on your particular circumstances. Having an attorney (professional third party) provides protection and respect for the parameters of the law. It essentially keeps everyone aware that they need to be open and forthright in sharing information.

In a recent *Institute of Divorce Financial Analyst* conference, a presenting family law judge stated that there is a minimum of six hearings in any divorce case, which is extremely expensive for each party, and she personally appreciates it when there is a financial expert involved to explain the tax implications and the details of the segregation of assets. Most attorneys and judges are not financial experts and appreciate clarification from knowledgeable professionals.

With a clear vision, necessary knowledge and guidance, we hope to empower you to make the best decisions for your particular situation and eliminate the possibility of future problems or the infamous gray areas that may haunt you for years to come. It is in everyone's best interest to ensure that all areas of your divorce agreement have been thoroughly addressed.

Since 95% of all divorce cases are settled out of court, wouldn't it be in your best interest to begin with The Collaborative Law Divorce Process?

CHAPTER 2
Personal Assessment

"Strange is our situation here upon earth. Each of us comes for a short visit, not knowing why, yet sometimes seeming to a divine purpose. From the standpoint of daily life, however, there is one thing we do know: That we are here for the sake of others...for the countless unknown souls with whose fate we are connected by a bond of sympathy. Many times a day, I realize how much my outer and inner life is built upon the labors of people, both living and dead, and how earnestly I must exert myself in order to give in return as much as I have received and am still receiving."

— Albert Einstein

Are you surprised that this is your reality? Are you concerned or fearful about your future? Are you so wrapped up in the process of divorce that you have not had a chance to look at your own life or future? While you may not know what your future holds, we encourage you to take the time to answer the questions in this personal assessment. There are no right or wrong answers. This process is just a building block to open your mind to the possibilities and provide encouragement and direction for a positive future.

This exercise will help you, your attorney, a CDFA and your divorce coach (if you choose) to help identify your priorities, fears, concerns, and allow you to plan accordingly. This information will be invaluable in ensuring that you and your attorney are negotiating based on your personal priorities for your current and long-term goals. In addition, there may be things that you are unaware of, and based on your unique individual situation, you can reprioritize to make this life transition easier. *Be prepared!* Your ability to effectively communicate your fears and concerns along with providing basic financial information *(Review Appendices C and D, and complete as much as you are able)* at your initial consultation will provide significant savings throughout the process.

PERSONAL ASSESSMENT

On a separate sheet of paper write down all of your responses
to share with your attorney, CDFA and divorce coach.

Skill and earning opportunity assessment:

- Are you currently employed? Is your job full-time or part-time?
- Are you the primary income provider?
- Do you own your own business?
- Are there issues related to the separation, ownership or duties of a family business?
- Does your job have opportunities for career advancement?
- Was your career primarily established as a source for secondary income?
- What skills or level of education do you have?
- If not working, how long have you been out of the workforce?
- Are there classes you need to take to update your skills or pursue a new career?
- Is your current job fulfilling, or would you prefer to do something else?
- What is most important to you in your job?

- Do you have any health issues that would impact your ability to hold or secure a job?
- Based on your age, level of education or health, is there any concern about your future income potential?

Values and Priorities:

Children:

- How many children do you have?
- Are there any health or learning issues with the children?
- Will you need childcare?
- Has the children's education been provided for?
- Will the children's lifestyle or activities change dramatically as a result of the divorce?
- What do you want most for your children?

While each state has different guidelines for child support expenses, there are inevitably many additional extraordinary expenses related to their upbringing; these expenses can be addressed in mediation or with your attorney regardless of the state in which you live. *See Appendix D for sample budget of some additional children's expenses.*

Home:

- Do you have funds to purchase a separate residence, or will you have to rent?
- Would it be financially prudent to have one party stay in the marital home?
- Is there equity in your home?
- If you have not worked and you sell your home, research the loan criteria for obtaining a new home. (There is usually an amount of time necessary to establish consistent income before monies are loaned.)

Money:

- Is there an adequate amount of money to meet each party's cash flow projections as documented in their personal budgets or financial affidavits?
- Are there any separate marital assets?
- Are there specific outstanding debts that are of concern?
- Are there significant health issues and related costs?

Retirement:

- Are there any retirement accounts?
- Are you aware of your social security benefits and rights?
- Are you aware of any pension benefits that exist through your employer or that of your spouse?
- Does either party have a family trust that would provide for their future expenses?

Personal Development:

- Are there courses you need to update or reactivate any degrees or certifications?
- Do you have continuing education requirements to fulfill?
- Are there courses in which you are interested?
- Have you done any research on classes or areas of interest?

By taking the time to answer the questions above and sharing your priorities with your attorney, he/she will be able to negotiate more successfully for you. We have also included in the appendices personal financial information that will be required in any divorce proceeding. *See Appendix C – Checklists and Worksheets and Appendix D – Budget for Additional Children's Expenses.*

To help you understand the value of this process, please review the following example:

CASE SCENARIO:

Tom and Mary decided to get a divorce after 15 years of marriage. They have two children, ages 13 and 14, and Mary has not worked in 10 years.

They have the following marital assets:

Savings	$20,000
Equity in Marital Home	$65,000
401k – Mary	$45,000
401k – Tom	$230,000
Deferred Compensation Plan – Tom	$79,000
Total Marital Assets:	**$439,000**

Situation #1: Based on the above scenario, there will not be much working capital for either party after the divorce. Mary has indicated that she would like to remain in the marital home for the sake of the children until they are 18 because they are in a good school district, and one of her biggest concerns is how they were going to pay for college.

Tom has agreed to allow Mary to remain in the marital home with the hopes that the home will appreciate and that the future equity will be used to pay for college. Upon sale of the marital home, a portion of the equity will be put in a separate account for educational expenses only. This allows Mary to get established in a career, provides stability for the children and minimizes stress over future educational expenses. Tom likes the idea that there is a way to save money, allow Mary to get established and provide for future needs without stress.

This is a very basic example of how the needs of each party can be met, while providing benefits to each in the short-term and long-term for the entire family unit.

Situation #2: Based on the same information above, Mary has not worked in 10 years and needs a few more classes to complete her degree. Tom does not have the extra income available to pay rehabilitative income but realizes it is in the best interest of the whole family that Mary complete her degree and get back to work full-time. Tom has allowed Mary to take an additional $30,000 of his 401k so that Mary can exercise her rights under Section 72 of the IRS code, which will allow Mary to take a withdrawal without having to pay the 10% early withdrawal penalty, and she can use this money to pay for her educational expenses. Also, after 4 years, her alimony will be reduced by a set amount. Tom is able to reduce his future alimony payments and reimburse his 401k.

This is another basic example of how **The Collaborative Law Divorce Process** can work. By being strategic and creative, both parties can achieve their goals in a fair and equitable manner that is in the best interests of the entire family.

The couples were able to achieve their personal goals because the parties took the time to ask questions and communicate. This is the crux of **The Collaborative Law Divorce Process**. Under a traditional divorce scenario, each party would have had a lawyer and typically the assets would be separated 50/50 and there would be much discussion as to the amount of spousal support needed and expenses of the children for years to come. This would only continue the adversarial relationship, which is not healthy for anyone.

No matter what circumstances ended the marriage, the collaborative law professionals are trained to promote compromise and resolution. Communication is paramount. When caught up in your own emotional turmoil or anger, it can be difficult to communicate effectively. In most cases, the lack of communication is what brought on the demise of most marriages. This further emphasizes the need for legal representation that can act in your best interests and why **The Collaborative Law Divorce Process** is the most beneficial. Collaborative law professionals receive additional training to obtain resolution even in the most difficult of cases. *When there is discord or distrust, promoting each party's interest is received much better when the ideas or options are presented or delivered* *by a trusted professional third party.* This communication or sharing of information promotes compromise for mutually beneficial interests—not a personal agenda.

By being upfront with financial information and your personal interests and goals, this allows all parties to negotiate fairly. **The Collaborative Law Divorce Process** is intended to create a contract to dissolve your marriage in a manner that is fair and promotes the interests of each party based on unique circumstances. If either party is not forthcoming with information as deemed necessary, you will have trained professionals to advise you.

While you may not know what your future holds, surrounding yourself with professionals with good intentions as well as faith in yourself will give you strength to get through this difficult time.

"For I know the plans that I have for you," declares the Lord, "plans to prosper you and not to harm you, plans to give you hope and a future." **- Jeremiah 29:11**

PART II

Evaluating your needs and creating a fair and complete Separation Agreement or Memorandum of Understanding

CHAPTER 3
Agreements Related to Children

Agreements related to children are usually addressed first, as this is the first priority of the courts and usually the parties as well. Agreements related to children should be inclusive of current circumstances, anticipated as well as unanticipated future events. These items should be addressed as specifically as possible to avoid any further stress or aggravation. As years go by, priorities change, especially when parties remarry and have stepchildren or more children. We encourage you to be as specific as possible and account for possible contingencies. We cannot emphasize this enough, as arrangements related to the children require you and your former spouse to interact for years.

Child Support:

Child support calculations are based on the type of custody arrangements for the child or children and the income of the parents. Each state has specific guidelines and formulas for the determination of child support. For presentation purposes, the following terms and guidelines have been summarized based on information retrieved from the North Carolina (NC) Human Services website. The worksheets referenced below can be found online.

- *Primary Custody* is when a child or children reside with one parent for at least 243 nights during the year. Child support is calculated based on the proportional income of each parent, and the amount computed for the non-custodial parent is paid to the custodial parent as child support. In this scenario, the amount of child support obligation is determined by using Worksheet A.
- *Joint or Shared Physical Custody* requires that the child or children reside with each parent at least 123 nights during the year. Based on this type of custody arrangement, the amount of child support obligation is determined by using Worksheet B.
- *Split Custody* indicates that each parent has custody of one of their children. This type of arrangement would calculate the amount of child support obligation using Worksheet C. Worksheet B would be used if the parents share custody of any of the children and have primary or split custody of any other children.
- *Legal Custody* relates to the parent that has the right to make long-term decisions affecting the health, education and general welfare of the child. There is no statutory authority in NC, which specifically defines legal custody. There is, however, case law. It does not relate to day-to-day decisions, which may be a result of parenting style.

We have found that most of our clients and the general public do not have a clear understanding of what expenses child support covers. It is meant to cover the child's reasonable needs, such as food, shelter, clothing, and medical, but it is also meant to cover expenses, such as basic school fees, entertainment, recreational activities, medical and other needs accustomed to the standard of living of the child and parties separating. See NC General Statutes § 50-13.4. for further details. All 50 states have established child support guidelines to determine the amount of child support a parent may be required to pay. Child support ends at 18 or when a child graduates from high school. College expenses are not considered in NC, but some states have statutes or guidelines that address this expense.

> **The amount of expenses deemed to be reasonable and customary usually differs greatly than the expectations of most parents. This is why it is important to prepare a separate budget for your children's expenses, compare that to the amount of child support calculated and make separate agreements related to these additional expenses that are deemed necessary for your family.**

See Appendix D for a sample budget of additional children's expenses. NC does not have any guidelines for child-related expenses, such as private school tuition, college expenses, transportation expenses for the child between the parent's homes or other expenses as considered necessary by the children's parents.

Child support is generally established to cover the following expenses:

- Basic Necessities—Food, clothing, and shelter
- Medical Care
- Uninsured Medical Expenses
- Educational Fees—School fees, supplies, and related costs)
- Childcare
- Transportation/Travel—Car, bus, insurance, gas, and fees)

Additional child-related expenses that may be even more costly based on your familial choices include:

- Extracurricular Activities—Summer camps, sport activities, travel and more
- Tutoring

- School Field Trips
- Summer Camps
- Entertainment
- Preparatory Fees and Registrations
- College Expenses—Some states have laws related to these expenses.

Each of these items can vary a greatly based on each child's needs and circumstances.

Personal Priorities:

- What expenses are of most concern to you related to your children?
- What expense items could you eliminate if needed?
- Do your children have any special needs: learning disabilities or health issues?

Items to Consider:

- Whether you have been a stay-at-home parent or the primary-income provider, you realize the time and energy it takes to positively support and parent your children. As a single parent, this task will become more taxing.
- Consider how your life will change and how you will accommodate and manage a new schedule.
- Your life may be changing greatly if you did not previously have a job. Consider how you will manage your time and still manage your home.
- Make sure you allow for rejuvenation time so that you can be the best parent you can be.
- When settling your agreement, no matter what has been agreed to, child support will always be modifiable. Please consult with your attorney for further information.

Examples of Child Support Arrangements:

Example 1 Sample Clause:

Husband shall pay to Wife child support in the amount of $_____ per month. The first of said payments shall be due and payable on the first day of the month following the execution of this Agreement and on the first day of each and every month thereafter until the occurrence of the first of the following contingencies:

1. Death of Husband
2. Death of minor children
3. The children cease to reside with wife
4. The youngest child, assuming all other children have previously done so, attaining his/her 18th birthday except if the child is still in primary or secondary school when the child reaches age 18, support payments shall continue until the child graduates, otherwise ceases to attend school on a regular basis, fails to make satisfactory progress towards graduation, or reaches age 20, whichever comes first: or
5. The emancipation of the children

Notwithstanding the above, child support may be modified by the consent of the parties or as provided by law.

Evaluation: This agreement is simple and clear.

Example 2 Sample Clause:

Husband shall pay monthly child support to Wife in the amount of $_____. Payments shall be made by electronic funds transfer or other recurring bill-pay type payments including timely payments by husband using his personal checks. All payments shall be made on or before the 5th day of each month with the first payment due on the occurrence of the due date after Wife and Husband physically separate. In any month, Husband may, at his option, make two individual payments with 50% due on the 5th day of the month and the second payment due on the 20th of the month. In no case shall the total amount of payment due in any month occur later than the 20th of said month. *

When XXX- eldest child reaches the age of 18 or graduates High School, whichever occurs later, the child support payments shall adjust to $1200 per month. When XXX - second child reaches the age of 18 or graduates High School, whichever occurs later, the child support payments shall adjust to $800 per month. When XXX – youngest child reaches the age of 18 or graduates High School, whichever occurs later, the child support payments shall cease.

Evaluation: There should be set dates for the required child support payments. The payments should be transferred via electronic funds without option of checks. This would minimize conflicts over the receipt of payments, holding periods to have access to funds and eliminate any interaction between the parties.

Notes/questions for your attorney:

_____

_____

_____

_____

_____

Child Custody and Parenting Time:

This clause outlines the decision-making authority and the schedule for time-sharing arrangements that the parents will have after they separate. It is important to provide guidelines to avoid any unnecessary confusion. When children reach their teens, they may no longer desire to go back and forth between households or may want to have more flexibility even if they have a good relationship with each parent. Use your discretion here, as forcing this issue can cause resentment. Eventually, location and convenience of available friends will become a priority. Parenting styles and influence will also have a factor. Try not to compare yourself or say any disparaging remarks about the other party. Be the parent you want to be!

Personal Priorities:

- What is/are the age(s) of the child/children and any childcare needs?
- Is your job flexible, or does your job require a great deal of travel?
- Do you work from home or do you work late most nights?
- Are you available for carpooling or involvement in extracurricular activities?

Items to Consider:

- Understand that parenting styles will be different, and you can only control what happens when the children are under your supervision.
- Avoid being a built-in babysitter.
- You need time for yourself and your own pursuits.
- Being a single parent is very difficult.
- The children's lives are being disrupted as well and they may act out. Be patient with them.

Example 1 Sample Clause:

Husband and Wife shall exercise joint legal and physical custody of the minor children. Each parent will alternate weeks, from Sunday at 7:00 p.m. until the following Sunday at 7:00 p.m., or at such other times that the parties agree.

Holidays: Husband and Wife shall agree upon a shared holiday schedule which will accommodate each other's family traditions. In the event Husband and Wife cannot agree upon a specific schedule for a specific holiday, the following schedule, which shall supersede the regular visitation schedule, shall apply:

<u>Thanksgiving:</u> The children shall be with Wife from Wednesday at 6 p.m. through Sunday at 6 p.m. in all even years, and with Husband from Wednesday at 6 p.m. through Sunday at 6 p.m. in all odd years.

<u>Christmas:</u> Husband shall have the children from the last day of school before Christmas recess until 2 p.m. on Christmas Day in all even years, and Wife shall have the children from 2 p.m. on Christmas Day until 6 p.m. on New Year's Day in all even years.

Wife shall have the children from the last day of school before Christmas recess until 2 p.m. on Christmas Day in all odd years, and Husband shall have the children from 2 p.m. on Christmas Day until 6 p.m. on New Year's Day in all odd years.

<u>Easter:</u> The children shall be with Wife in all even years from the last day of school before the Easter recess at 6 p.m. until the day before school resumes at 6 p.m. The children shall be with Husband in all odd years from the last day of school before the Easter recess at 6 p.m. until the day before school resumes at 6 p.m.

<u>Mother's Day/Father's Day:</u> The children will always be with the honored parent from 7 p.m. on Saturday until 7 p.m. on Sunday.

Evaluation: The agreement might be a bit easier to manage if the language addressing transition from one home to another was changed to "from the time school dismisses for Thanksgiving, Christmas, etc. rather than at 6 p.m. as noted in the clause above. This agreement is very clear and concise. It allows for each parent to manage their time and vacations with the children without interference or interruption from the other parent.

<u>Example 2 Sample Clause:</u>

The parties recognize that the other is a fit, proper and loving party and is totally competent to provide for and care for their children when they are with either party. Accordingly, Husband and Wife have agreed to be "joint legal and joint physical" custodians for the parenting of their children.

Husband shall have the children every other weekend from 6:00 p.m. Thursday until he returns them to school on the following Monday morning. Husband shall also have the option of having the children from 6:00 – 9:00 p.m. on any Tuesday or Wednesday of each week ("flex day"). When Husband elects to use such a flex day, he shall notify Wife of his intentions no later than 6:00 p.m. Friday of the preceding week.

The following holiday schedules shall take precedence over the normal week-to-week schedule.

Memorial Day – This period begins 6:00 p.m. on the Friday before Memorial Day and ends when they are returned to school on the Tuesday following Memorial Day. Husband shall have the children during this time in even-numbered years and Wife shall have them in odd-numbered years. In the event that this time period falls on a weekend that normally belongs to the other parent, the other parent may select, and first parent shall forfeit, the weekend prior to or the weekend following Memorial Day as compensation for his or her lost time. In this case, the other parent shall notify the first parent as to which weekend shall be forfeited at least 30 days prior to the commencement of that weekend.

Labor Day - This period begins 6:00 p.m. on the Friday before Labor Day and ends when they are returned to school on the Tuesday following Labor Day. Husband shall have the children during this time in odd-numbered years and Wife shall have them in even-numbered years. In the event that this time period falls on a weekend that normally belongs to the other parent, the other parent may select, and first parent shall forfeit, the weekend prior to or the weekend following Labor Day as compensation for his or her lost time. In this case, the other parent shall notify the first parent as to which weekend shall be forfeited at least 30 days prior to the commencement of that weekend.

Father's Day – In all years, Husband shall have the children from 8:00 a.m. Sunday – 8:00 a.m. Monday.

Mother's Day - In all years, Wife shall have the children from 8:00 a.m. Sunday – 8:00 a.m. Monday.

Spring Break – The parent owning the weekend before this time shall have the children from 8:00 a.m. Monday until 12:00 noon Wednesday and the other parent shall have the children from 12:00 noon Wednesday until 6:00 p.m. Friday.

Halloween - This time period begins at 4:00 p.m. and ends at 10:00 p.m. Wife shall have the children during this time in all years. Additionally, the parents agree that they notify each other as to the children's whereabouts so that each parent will have the opportunity to spend time with them. Lastly, the parents agree that neither will attempt to place restrictions on each other if either wishes to spend time with the children while they are outdoors in any neighborhood or in another public place.

Child's birthday – The parents agree that the parent hosting the children overnight on a child's birthday shall coordinate a family gathering at a neutral location at a time when both parents may attend. In the event the parent coordinating the event is unwilling to attend with the other parent there, the coordinating parent shall forfeit the time to the parent who wishes to attend. The parent coordinating the gathering shall exercise his or her best effort to maximize the potential for the other parent to attend.

Mother's Birthday – In all years, Mother shall have the option of having the children from 4:00 – 8:00 p.m. if her birthday falls on a weekday and from 8:00 a.m. to 8:00 p.m, if her birthday falls on a weekend.

Thanksgiving – This time period begins when the children are dismissed from school on the last day prior to the break and ends when they are returned to school at the end of the break. Husband shall have the children in even-numbered years and Wife shall have them in odd-numbered years.

Christmas – In odd-numbered years, Husband shall have the children from 6:00 p.m. December 23 until 10:00 a.m. December 25 and Wife shall then have them from 10:00 a.m. December 25 until 10:00 a.m. December 27. In even-numbered years, Wife shall have the children from 6:00 p.m. December 23 until 10:00 a.m. December 25 and Husband shall then have them from 10:00 a.m. December 25 until 10:00 a.m. December 27. In odd- numbered years, Husband shall have the option of traveling with the children for any length of time from 8:00 a.m. December 22 until 11:00 p.m. December 28. Wife will have the same option in even-numbered years. The travelling parent shall notify the other parent of his or her intentions of travel at least 30 days prior to the commencement of such travel.

New Year's Eve/New Year's Day – This time period begins 10:00a.m. December 31 and ends 6:00 p.m. January 1. Husband shall have the children during this time in odd-numbered years and Wife shall have them in even –numbered years.

Evaluation: This agreement is very specific due to the adversarial relationship between the parents. This amount of detail is also important for children of a young age to prepare for events without stress and confusion.

Notes/questions for your attorney:

_____

_____

_____

_____

_____

Health Insurance – There is a line item on the child support worksheet (in NC) that factors the cost of health insurance premiums attributable to the child or children. If either party has health coverage, it would be prudent to compare policies to determine which policy offers the best cost and features needed for your child's/children's needs. <u>There are many expenses that are not considered in the child support calculation related to medical coverage, such as co-pays and deductibles. Ensure that your agreement takes into account how these expenses and any other unanticipated healthcare expenses will be paid and by whom.</u>

Personal Priorities:

- Does your child/children have chronic health issues?
- Is your child active or does he/she play on sport teams? Some kind of injury is likely to occur.
- Is your job flexible enough to accommodate doctor visits or sick days when your child must miss school?
- Do you have help in case of an emergency?

Items to Consider:

- Each parent's ability to obtain a reasonably priced plan.
- The rising costs of healthcare as well as the related premiums.
- Uninsured costs such as annual deductibles and out of network expenses.

Example 1 Sample Clause:

Husband shall, as additional child support, maintain and pay for a policy of major medical and hospitalization insurance for the benefit of the minor children. Husband and wife shall be responsible for and the discharge one-half of all uninsured medical, dental, orthodontic, optometric, prescription and other such expenses incurred on behalf of said children.

For uninsured expenses, the party incurring the expense shall furnish to the other party proof of such expense within thirty (30) days of the expense being incurred. The other party shall reimburse the party incurring the expense within thirty (30) days of receiving proof of the expense.

Example 2 Sample Clause:

The children will remain on Husband's medical/dental/mental health/ vision policy and Husband shall pay their premiums. Regardless as to in which policy the children are enrolled, Husband shall pay the first $5,000. 00 of expenses that are not covered by insurance.

In the event health insurance benefits are no longer available through Husband's employer and Wife has a policy available to her, the children shall be placed on that policy and the Wife shall pay the premiums. If Wife has no policy available, Husband and Wife shall acquire a private policy for the children and they will equally share the cost of the associated premiums and medical costs that are not covered by the plan.

Neither parent shall obtain medical care from a provider outside of the network in which the children are enrolled unless both agree in advance of the service being provided or in case of an emergency and network providers are unavailable.

Notes/questions for your attorney:

_____

_____

_____

_____

_____

Children's Education and College Savings Accounts:

A detailed list including all account numbers and types of child savings accounts should be outlined in your divorce agreement. Identify who will maintain and be custodian thereof. Make sure any agreed-to changes are made prior to signing of your Separation and Property Settlement Agreement. In many states, the parents are not legally obligated to provide for college expenses. While most parents would agree that this is a necessary expense, many are not willing to compromise on the payment thereof or agree to it in writing. Determine if there will be contributions required and ensure that the timing and frequency of those payments be clearly outlined.

Personal Priorities:

- Most parents want their children to go to college and intend to assist them in some way. Discuss scenarios with your attorney and/or CDFA/CPA to ensure there is a clear understanding of how these agreed-upon expenses will be paid.
- The choice of school the child attends may be of importance to either party.

Items to Consider:

- Is there enough cash to pay for the children's college needs?
- If additional monies are needed, how will this be addressed?

Example 1 Sample Clause:

If and in the event the minor children desire to pursue a higher education after completed high school, the actual cost (tuition, books, room, board and other fees normally charged by the institution) for such higher education, not exceeding the cost of said education then in effect at the University of North Carolina at Chapel Hill, North Carolina for North Carolina residents, shall be borne equally by Husband and Wife. In addition, Husband and Wife shall afford such children reasonable sums to be determined by Husband and Wife for transportation, clothing and spending allowances considering the earnings of the children. The obligation of Husband to afford the children with a higher education as aforesaid shall be limited to undergraduate school, and if the children fail to graduate within the normal period for the course of study undertaken within the regular period not in excess of four (4) years, then the Husband and Wife at their option, may cease further payment to or for the benefit of such children.

Husband is owner of two (2) College Funds (529 Plans), which have a balance of approximately $100,000.00. Said 529 plans shall remain in Husband's name with Wife listed as successor. Husband and Wife stipulate and agree that the Plans shall first be applied to college expenses for the minor children. Any remaining balance shall be distributed equally to Husband and Wife.

Evaluation: This agreement is very clear and concise. It addresses maximum costs to be borne by each party and allows each party to contribute what they each deem reasonable for transportation, living and other spending allowances.

Example 2 Sample Clause:

The established 529 college savings accounts shall be used for the respective child's college education. Investment decisions for these accounts shall be made jointly and neither parent shall have final authority over such decisions. If the parents later negotiate an acceptable college cost sharing plan, these funds shall credit to each parent's responsibility equally. In the event the parents are unable to negotiate an acceptable cost sharing plan for college, each fund shall be equally shared by the parents at the time the respective child commences college. The parties shall jointly decide upon any withdrawals from these accounts.

Evaluation: It is not recommended that the parents continue to make joint decisions. There is bound to be controversy related to these choices. Be specific on what the funds will be used for, how extra costs will be determined and paid for. If circumstances change and there are excess funds then the distribution of these funds should be clearly stated.

Notes/questions for your attorney:

_____

_____

_____

_____

_____

Life Insurance – Since child support payments usually terminate upon the death of the payor or can be reduced if the payor becomes disabled, each party should consider having a life/disability insurance policy or a term policy as deemed necessary based on the each party's circumstances. Life insurance is usually purchased to protect against loss of income for the payment of alimony and/or child support. This is a very important clause to consider.

Personal Priorities:

- Do I have protection for future payments if spouse dies or becomes disabled?
- Is there life insurance provided or purchased through a former spouse's company?
- Can there be an irrevocable beneficiary assignment?
- Is a separate policy needed?
- Do I have enough income to pay for myself and the children if my former spouse dies or becomes disabled?

Items to Consider:

- It is best to have the beneficiary of the policy also be the owner of the policy. This will ensure that the premiums are being paid timely and that there will be no unauthorized changes to the beneficiary.
- Based on the age, circumstances and length of time that coverage is needed will determine the priority of having life insurance.

<u>Example 1 Sample Clause:</u>

Husband shall maintain a life insurance policy on both Husband's and Wife's lives naming Wife as beneficiary of Husband's insurance policy and Husband as beneficiary of Wife's insurance policy thereof in trust for the said minor children. Husband's obligation to maintain said coverage shall continue for so long as he has an obligation to provide the minor children with support or a college education as herein provided. The obligation of Husband to maintain said insurance shall be a charge upon his estate. Husband shall furnish to Wife upon request proof of existence of said coverage, including a copy of said insurance policies.

Evaluation: The agreement should also state the policy numbers, amount and type of policy purchased. Depending on the type of policy purchased, term or whole life, there may be other items to consider. Typically, life insurance is on the life of the primary income provider. If both parties work and have comparable income, then two policies are usually considered.

It is usually recommended to allow for a decrease in the death benefit designation as the support obligations are satisfied. It is also recommended that there is a provision that allows each party access to information regarding coverage and beneficiary information directly from the provider. There are forms that can be signed permitting an interested party to have access to the coverage and beneficiary information. Ensure that these documents are obtained and approved by the provider before signing your final agreement.

<u>Example 2 Sample Clause:</u>

Husband shall carry a life insurance policy or group policies with an aggregate benefit of $1,000,000.00 on himself until July 30, 2018. The primary beneficiary of this level of death benefit shall be Wife. In the event Wife requests evidence of insurance that demonstrates Husband's compliance with this provision, Husband shall provide such evidence within 14 days of the request. Husband may name any secondary beneficiaries of his choosing.

Wife shall carry a life insurance policy or group policies with an aggregate benefit of $1,000,000.00 on herself until July 30, 2018. The primary beneficiary of this level of death benefit shall be Husband. In the event Husband requests evidence of insurance that demonstrates Husband's compliance with this provision, Wife shall provide such evidence within 14 days of the request. Husband may name any secondary beneficiaries of his choosing.

Evaluation: In order to avoid any further communication or to ensure that the said policies are being maintained, each beneficiary should be the owner of the policy from which they would benefit. Again, the dollar amount of the policies, access to policy information and death benefit designations should be in align with the circumstances of each couple.

Notes/questions for your attorney:

_____

_____

_____

_____

_____

> **The clauses listed below are very general in nature, but may be important if applicable to your circumstances. While many provide a general understanding, it is important to note that these clauses will probably be violated in some form and the cost, time and energy to enforce these clauses usually will not provide any benefit.**

Relocation – Many careers require relocation for advancement and/or significant travel. If there is a chance that either parent anticipates that this may be an issue for him/her, we have provided the following sample clause for your consideration.

In the event that either party wishes to relocate with the child or children more than XXXX miles away from the other parent's residence, consider what new arrangements (cost of travel, details of new arrangements) should be made that would be agreeable to either party.

Personal Priorities:
- Will your career require you to move to advance your career?
- Would it be easier to be near family so you can go back to work?

Items to Consider:
- As parties remarry, there may be a need for a move or significant relocation.
- A sole legal custody arrangement may cause issues if only one parent has legal authority to make decisions on behalf of the child/children.

Sample Clause:

Unless the parties otherwise agree in writing which is signed and notarized, the following shall occur:

In the event either party wishes to relocate with the children more than 30 miles away from the other parent's residence, the first parent shall, as soon as possible, notify the other parent of his or her intentions in writing and will not relocate until a new time-sharing agreement is negotiated or is ordered by a court of law. The parents agree that once written notification is given, they shall, in good faith, actively participate in negotiating a new time sharing agreement according to the following timeline:

Self-negotiation (parent to parent)   14 days from date of notification
Negotiation through mediation   25 days from date of notification

Lastly, the parent remaining shall not relocate with the children to any location that takes them out of their current school district until the new time sharing plan is established and neither parent shall relocate with the children outside of the continental United States.

Evaluation: There is specific case law, which deals with relocation issues. Regardless of the sole or joint legal custody, a relocation which, requires a change in the implementation of the parenting agreement must be shown to be in the best interests of the child. No relocation will be allowed if it is done for spiteful purposes.

Notes/questions for your attorney:

Extracurricular Activities- This clause relates to any extracurricular activities that the children may have an interest in or that the parents or one parent may deem appropriate. Many children are extremely active and participate in numerous sports, clubs and religious or cultural activities. These activities can be expensive and are not always given the same priority by both parents. This clause provides an outline of the types of expenses that could occur and who will be responsible for payment and participation.

Personal Priorities:

- There may be limited amount of funds available and the activities will have to be prioritized.
- Some activities may be considered of more value or more necessary than others. Consideration should be given to all parties involved as well as the child's/children's desire to participate in such activity.

Items to Consider:

- There may be health issues that should be addressed if child has had injuries; concussions, surgeries, asthma, etc.

Sample Clause:

All decisions relating to the suitability of participation in extracurricular activities shall be made jointly and neither parent shall have final authority over such decisions. The parents shall not make plans or schedule activities for the children that will impinge on the other party's designated time without the other parent's prior consent. The activities addressed in this paragraph refer to those such as, but not limited to, sports, travel, lessons, camps (for non-work related day care purposes), youth trips, and other similar types of activity.

When it is agreed that a proposed expense is appropriate for the children, the respective cost shall be shared equally and either parent may refrain from paying for any further costs once the children's total combined monthly expenditures exceeds $500.00 per parent per month. If, however, a parent's only objection to a specific activity proposed by the other parent is the cost of the activity, the proposing parent shall have the option of allowing their children to participate in the activity at their individual expense without the other parent being required to make a financial contribution toward the cost of the activity.

Notes/questions for your attorney:

_____
_____
_____
_____
_____

Reconciliation of Shared Expenses – If there are significant expenses related to the child's/children's activities, lessons and/or other extracurricular activities that are deemed in excess of the child support amount, then details of these expenditures and how they will be paid should be outlined in as much detail as possible. The child support guidelines only go up to cumulative income of $25,000 per month ($300,000 per year). Income in excess of this sum is outside of the guidelines and is then based on the needs of the child/children but must be at least the highest sum under the guidelines. Many who do not have this amount of income find that their current spending for their child/ children exceed the child support calculations and negotiate shared costs arrangements for the estimated excess costs.

Sample Clause:

Agreed upon educational expenses such as tutoring, school uniforms, school supplies and activity fees shall be shared equally but shall be included in the limits as previously defined above.

Each parent shall save paid receipts reflecting any expense that each pays for the benefit of the children. Reconciliation shall take place once a month and reimbursement to the parent who has overpaid shall be paid on or before the 15th of every month.

Notes/questions for your attorney:

_____

_____

_____

_____

_____

Dependency Exemptions - Usually the spouse paying child support requests to be able to claim exemptions on the child/children. If cash flow is tight, there may be options to be considered that would provide excess cash depending on the tax bracket of the parties involved. Depending on the income level of each spouse, there are child-related tax credits that may be taken advantage of for the mutual benefit of both parties.

Personal Priorities:
- Ensure that the maximum benefit is received.

Items to Consider:

- It is recommended to consult with your tax advisor to understand your rights.
- Each party can alternate claiming dependent exemptions; this may be accomplished by preparing IRS form 8332 annually.

Example 1 Sample Clause:

Wife shall be entitled to the dependency exemption allowable under Section 151(e) of the Internal Revenue Code during the minority of child 1 and for so long as dependency exemption is allowable under the Internal Revenue Code as well as for North Carolina state income tax purposes and for so long as dependency exemption is allowable under North Carolina law.

Husband shall be entitled to the dependency exemption allowable under Section 151(e) of the Internal Revenue Code during the minority of child 2 and for so long as dependency exemption is allowable under the Internal Revenue Code as well as for North Carolina state income tax purposes and for so long as dependency exemption is allowable under North Carolina law.

Example 2 Sample Clause:

In tax year 2015 and future odd-numbered tax years, Wife will claim all children as dependents on their respective Federal and State returns. In tax year 2016 and future even-numbered tax years, Husband will claim all children as dependents on their respective Federal and State returns. The parents agree to sign any necessary IRS forms to facilitate this assignment of dependency.

Notes/questions for your attorney:

_____

_____

_____

_____

_____

Vacation and Travel – There may be concerns over travel outside of the United States or the state of residence. This clause ensures that proper communication about the whereabouts of the children is made available to either party to avoid unnecessary emotional stress and concern. There may be other items to consider if there is a threat that your child/children may be brought to another country if not agreed upon. Consult with your attorney.

Sample Clause:

If Husband or Wife wishes to travel with any of their children outside of the United States, the other parent must first be in agreement to the destination and conditions of the trip. Once they have agreed, to the trip, they shall co-operate in obtaining the necessary documents for the children to obtain passports.

If either parent schedules travel away with the children that requires an overnight absence away from that parent's home, that parent shall notify the other parent as soon as the absence is planned and provide the other parent with an itinerary and contact information before any trip commences.

Notes/questions for your attorney:

_____

_____

_____

_____

_____

Spiritual Development – This clause is purely dependent on the priority the parties want to put on this area. This may be something you agreed to when you were married or when you had your child/children.

Sample Clause:

The children shall be raised catholic. All other major religious training decisions will be made jointly and neither parent shall have final authority over such decisions. However, the parent with whom the children are residing at the time may make immediate, short-term decisions concerning their religious training needs and will notify the other parent within 24 hours.

Notes/questions for your attorney:

_____

_____

_____

_____

_____

Incapacitated Child or Children – This is a standard clause in most agreements to ensure that each party is aware of the physical and financial responsibility in this event relates to your child.

Sample Clause:

The parties have been advised that pursuant to the North Carolina General Statutes 50-13.8, they may be liable for the continuing support of any of their children that are mentally or physically incapable of self-supporting upon reaching majority and continuing for so long as said incapacity exists.

General Parenting Issues and Discipline:

Example 1 Sample Clause:

Husband and Wife shall consult together frequently in an effort to agree concerning the general health, education and development of the minor children to the end that they adopt a harmonious policy in regard to the children's upbringing.

Evaluation: This is admirable but not considered necessary. It acts as a reminder to be considerate of each parent's role in their children's lives. The cost benefit of enforcing this clause is negligible.

Example 2 Sample Clause:

Husband and Wife will continue with their respective parenting and discipline styles and thresholds to which the children are currently accustomed. If either parent was to have an issue with the way the other parent disciplines the children, they will discuss the issue to find an agreeable solution.

Neither, Husband or Wife shall permit any significant romantic interest, fiancé, or spouse to offer additional privileges, rewards, or gifts that are not normally provided by Husband or Wife without prior permission.

Evaluation: Again, while this may have good intentions, the cost benefit of enforcing this clause is negligible.

Notes/questions for your attorney:

_____

_____

_____

_____

_____

Communication and Ethics – This is a clause that is usually documented so that both parties will have a general understanding of the other's priorities as they make a new life for themselves. Many of these items may change as other spouses and children enter the family units. If things are not handled as originally discussed or documented, try to do your best to set boundaries and manage your children as you determine is in their best interest. You no longer have a say in the decisions or actions made in the other household, unless there is threat of physical harm or abuse. What you believe to be ethical may very well differ from your ex-spouse and his/her family. Do your best to communicate effectively, and not play games. It may be in your best interest to limit interaction to emails or always have a third-party present for any communication.

Example 1 Sample Clause:

Husband and Wife shall consult together frequently in an effort to agree concerning the general health, education and development of the minor children to the end that they adopt a harmonious policy in regard to the children's upbringing insofar as possible. The parties agree to consult with one another concerning the children's college education and the children's (and parents) selection of a college. Neither party shall attempt, or condone any attempt, directly or indirectly, to estrange the children from the other party or to injure or impair the love and affection between parent and children. The parties shall at all times encourage and foster in the children sincere respect and affection for both parents. Each party shall immediately advise the other as to any serious illness or other major development with respect to the children. Each parent shall be entitled to immediate access from the other, or from a third party, to records and information pertaining to the minor children, including but not limited to, medical, dental, health, school or educational records. Each party shall be entitled to speak to the children by telephone at reasonable times and intervals when the children are with the other party

Example 2 Sample Clause:

Husband and Wife have determined that they will jointly decide many issues relating to the children. In such situations where they cannot agree, the current practice shall remain in effect.

The parents shall support each other in their roles as parents and shall take into account the views of the other for the physical and mental wellbeing of the children. They shall at all times keep each other timely informed as to the children. They shall at all times keep each other informed of children's appointments, meetings, programs, performances, game activities, and other events. If a parent has doubt as to the importance of such event, that parent shall notify the other as soon as the event is scheduled.

Neither parent shall intentionally do anything that would estrange the children from the other parent or impair the natural development of their love and respect for each parent, possible stepparents, siblings or other extended family members. In addition, the parents will not discuss time sharing issues or disagreements in the presence of the children.

Evaluation: Both of these clauses are very clear and concise and are typical of most agreements. In many cases this clause will be violated countless times. Do your best to focus on what you can control. Many of these issues would be hard to contest or rectify after the action was already taken.

Notes/questions for your attorney:

_____

_____

_____

_____

_____

Miscellaneous Parenting – If there is anything specific to your lifestyle or circumstances that you have concerns about, this is where those items should be documented.

Example Sample Clause:

A. All decisions relating to major appearance changes shall be made jointly in advance and neither parent shall have the final authority over such decisions. Examples of appearance changes are piercings, significant change in hair length, tattoos, or any other change that presents a permanent or semi-permanent result.

B. All decisions relating to the acquiring of a driver's license or learner's permit and the use or ownership of an automobile shall be made jointly in advance and neither parent shall have final authority over such decisions.

C. The children shall not be permitted to ride upon a motorcycle of any type at any time.

D. The children shall not be permitted to ride upon an ATV of any type at any time unless that child is under the direct supervision of the father. Appropriate protective gear shall always be worn while riding.

Evaluation: Please note that this clause is specific to your personal situation.

Notes/questions for your attorney:

_____

_____

_____

_____

_____

Conclusion:

When discussing the details of child support, we recommend that the parties have a clear understanding of what expenses are expected to be covered by child support and document other expenses as known or anticipated. These other expenses should be addressed and a clear plan outlined in your agreement for these extraordinary costs. ***See Appendix D – Budget for Additional Children's Expenses.*** This will help to avoid controversy in the years to come. Anything related to a monetary commitment should be documented in detail.

Other clauses related to decision making, general well-being, parenting and spiritual development should be documented to serve as a basis for the parties general understanding. These agreements will inevitably be violated in some way. Save yourself the time and aggravation of this stress by acknowledging this fact and return your focus to items that can be controlled.

As children grow, they will have their own perspectives and seek independence in numerous ways. Determine your own priorities and proceed accordingly. Try to refrain from insulting or disparaging your former spouse in any way. This will pay dividends in the long run. Again, there will be numerous factors that are no longer in your control. Your family dynamic and relationship with your child/children will be affected by this change in structure and parental involvement. Many children rebel or act out because they are hurting inside themselves. This presents yet another stress to your life that can be very difficult. We recommend that you encourage your child/children to have a relationship with a friend or relative that can assist if needed. If circumstances are more serious, there are many experienced family therapists that specialize in this area. We recommend that you interview and meet with these professionals to understand the process and find a good fit for your family.

CHAPTER 4
Agreements Related to Marital Assets

Marital Assets includes anything accumulated (there are certain exceptions as determined by your state's statutes) or acquired during the length of the marriage. Marital assets also include any gifts or inheritance received during the marriage by either party when these assets are put into a joint account or used to purchase joint property. If these assets/monies were received during the marriage and kept in a separate account, these assets would be considered separate property and would not be included in the list of marital assets subject to allocation between the two parties. Although, the interest earned or gained on these separate assets may be considered marital property.

The division of property in divorce cases is determined by the statutes of the state in which the couple resides. There are community property or equitable distribution property division statutes. Community property states generally provide for a 50/50 split of the marital assets. Equitable distribution states generally try to make a fair allocation of marital assets based on the couple's circumstances.

Whether you are mediating or using the traditional divorce litigation process, there will be an intense negotiation over what is fair and equitable. On the surface, an equal split of the assets may appear to be fair, but this presentation of the assets can be deceiving when you consider the types of assets that are being allocated. Are these assets appreciating or depreciating? In other words, does the asset appreciate on its own, or will the asset require cash to maintain? What are the tax implications upon liquidation?

By reviewing the current and long-term effects of how the marital assets could be separated and then analyzing the monthly cash available for child support and alimony, there are *many options* to be considered that would allow for a fair and equitable agreement while maximizing cash flow opportunities. ***See Appendix A*** for a case scenario that exemplifies these statements.

Another significant item to consider is outstanding debt. It is best to eliminate any joint debt prior to separation. It is imperative that any outstanding debts be paid in full or refinanced solely under one party before your divorce agreement is signed. *No matter what your divorce agreement may say, both parties are still liable for debt incurred during the marriage.* This process begins by each party preparing an affidavit listing their assets and liabilities. In many cases, the other party may not even be aware of the assets or outstanding liabilities they jointly own. It is recommended to have a credit report run on each party to ensure full disclosure.

If there is any question about adequate financial disclosure or the ability to gather the necessary information, we recommend that you consult with your attorney. We also recommend the use of a CDFA to ensure all financial information received is accurate, all assets and liabilities are accounted for and financial allocation options are communicated.

When segregating marital assets, the listing of assets is usually shown at retail or fair market value, even though the after-tax value can be significantly different. When there are two assets of equal face value, but with a wide discrepancy in the basis of each, the taxable gains on each asset can make their values quite unequal

upon liquidation. These differences should be addressed when negotiating your settlement.

Dividing the property can be one of the most challenging and convoluted aspects of a divorce. What appears to be an easy decision, such as "I want the house, and you keep the cars," may in the end deliver a settlement nobody had intended.

> **Listed below are examples of typical marital assets. For each asset, we have provided a general explanation, personal priorities, items to consider, real situations, sample legal clauses and evaluation thereof.**

Real Estate: In most instances, the marital home is the largest asset that a couple has to divide. There are many options to consider based on your personal situation of whether to sell the home, transfer ownership or allow one party to remain for a set amount of time. If the home is not going to be sold, then the related mortgage should be refinanced in the party's name who will be receiving this asset. If you are entertaining the idea of one party living in the home for a set period of time or if you have been separated for a significant period of time, there are special tax rules relating to divorce (including use period, ownership period and capital gain exclusions) that should be addressed.

Personal Priorities:
- There is little to no equity in the home.
- There are children from the marriage and it would be less disruptive for the custodial parent to remain in the home.
- One party cannot qualify to rent or purchase a home on his/her own without a historical proof of income.
- One party is emotionally attached to the home.
- A rental property is converted to a primary residence.

Items to Consider:

When there is little to no equity in the home, the parties will need to consider future cash flow needs and the desire of one spouse to assume risk/liability of the home and its future economic recovery. There may be other circumstances when it is appropriate for one party to remain in the marital home for a certain period of time. The splitting of this asset under any of these circumstances can have many implications.

If it is determined that one party may choose to live in the marital home for a set period of time in hopes of recovering his/her investment, the agreement needs to be very specific about how the proceeds will be split and how the costs to maintain this asset will be approved, paid and/or allocated upon sale at a future date. Both parties should be on the deed to avoid any tax issues when the home is sold at a later date. Be sure to review tax laws related to ownership and use to ensure your clause is in accordance with federal regulations, as these rules take precedence over any items that may have been agreed to in your divorce agreement. Details of this arrangement should be specific to avoid future stress and chaos.

If one party chooses to buy out the other party, then the parties should agree on how the asset should be valued and how the asset can be refinanced in the purchasing party's name. Before entertaining this option, it must be determined if the bank would approve the refinanced mortgage based on one party's sole income. If the mortgage and deed are already in the name of the spouse keeping the asset, no further action is required. If the mortgage is in the name of the spouse keeping the asset, but the deed is in both party's names, then the deed can be transferred via a Quit Claim Deed. If both names are on the mortgage and the deed, then the home should be refinanced in the purchasing party's name. Any equity in the home would then be considered when allocating other marital assets.

Many parties are emotionally attached to their homes. At first glance, one may think he/she is making a good decision by keeping the home, but after a few months or years he/she may find himself/herself are strapped for cash and will incur additional moving costs, realtor fees and closing costs to move at a later date. Some parties may feel it is in the best interest of their children to remain in the marital home until the children reach a certain age. Also depending on the income of the parties, one party may be unable to purchase or rent without an established income, or it may be more costly than anticipated to do so. In these situations, the parties could entertain the possibility of one party remaining in the home for a set period of time until a financial income stream is established to allow both parties to move on in a fair and equitable fashion.

If one party receives rental property and chooses to sell it and purchase another home or desires to make it his/her primary residence, there will eventually be tax consequences based on the amount of depreciation taken and any losses incurred when the property is eventually sold. While this option can offer many benefits, it is important to understand the financial impact of these options before committing to the allocation at the time of the divorce. Long-term projections will help each party understand the financial impact of these types of allocations.

For example, Jane moves into the rental property in 2014 and lives there for 2 years before selling it in 2016. By the time she sells it, she has owned it for 17 years. Five of those 17 years, it was a rental property. To calculate her taxable gain, take the total number of years it was rented (5) divided by the total number of years owned (17). This percentage of rental period 5/17 = 29.4% will be applied to the gain on the sale. In addition, Jane will be taxed on the allowable depreciation taken as a rental property. The remaining 12/17 = 70.6% can be offset by the $250,000 capital gain exclusion.

Depending on how the marital home is allocated between the parties, it can have a direct impact on future alimony discussions as well. Based on the cash flow needs of each party and personal interest of the parties' situation, there are many considerations that would enable the parties to maximize cash flow and reduce stress. Be proactive and discuss your situation with your attorney and a CDFA; they can present options that can be mutually beneficial.

Based on a true story - One of our clients was divorcing her husband. The husband attempted to liquidate all funds related to a line of credit on their marital home to reimburse family members who had loaned them money throughout their marriage. There were no formal promissory notes and there were no other marital assets. He told his wife that he would file for divorce after the sale and closing of their marital home. Our client quickly contacted the bank to ensure no other monies would be dispersed, filed for a divorce and was able to prevent the remaining equity from being taken before an equitable property settlement agreement could be obtained.

Another true story – A woman was emotionally overwhelmed and chose to stay in her marital home until the children went to college and then the home would be sold. The woman depleted the majority of her alimony maintaining the marital home for herself and the children. In addition, the woman had to endure constant visits and interruption from her former spouse under the guise of maintaining his investment and visiting the children.

If one party chooses to stay in the marital home, there should be specific items outlined to ensure privacy and the right to live freely. Also, if either party plans on purchasing a home after separation but prior to the final divorce agreement having been filed, consult your attorney for a Free Trader Agreement to protect the investment.

Example 1 Sample Clause:

The parties are owners of real property and residence located at 809 Briar Lane, Camden, GA 45607. This property is encumbered by a note and deed of trust in favor of SunTrust with a principal balance of approximately $484,000.00 and monthly payments of approximately

$2,600.00. Simultaneously with the execution of this Agreement, the parties shall immediately list the residence for sale with an agreed upon realtor at an agreed upon fair market value. Husband and Wife will continue to reside in said residence pending the sale on an alternating weekly basis, with the party residing in the residence also having regular visitation with the minor children. The party residing in the residence shall be responsible for keeping the home in a clean and presentable fashion, at all times, suitable to be shown by a realtor. Any major repairs needed during this time will be deducted from the sale and reimbursed to the appropriate party before any proceeds are disbursed. Pending sale, Husband shall be responsible for and discharge all obligations in connection with the ownership of the said residence, including but not limited to the mortgage payments, taxes, insurance, homeowner's dues, maintenance and utilities. Upon sale of the residence, the parties agree to divide the net proceeds equally.

Evaluation: This agreement is clear and concise.

Example 2 Sample Clause:

There is a marital home located at 1544 Green Park Way, Charlotte, NC 28xxx. There is a first mortgage (Bank of America, #) in the amount of $299,851.00 and a second mortgage (BB&T, #) in the amount of $127,962.00. The deed and the mortgage are in both Husband and Wife's names. The parties will remain as joint owners of the residence until such a time that it is sold. Effective immediately, Husband shall be responsible for all costs associated with owning or living in the home, including, but not limited to, the timely payment of the first and second mortgages, taxes, insurance, utilities, homeowner's dues, and costs relating to the short-term maintenance such as yard upkeep.

Husband shall place the home for sale in the Multiple Listing Service on or before June 15, 20XX. Any decisions relating to the sale of the home including, but not limited to, selection of real estate agent, price setting, price reduction, or offer acceptance, shall be made by Husband.

However, Husband shall be obligated to accept any offer that is greater than $650,000. While the home is listed for sale, Husband shall maintain it in a "showable" condition at all times, not limiting access to potential buyers or agents during reasonable showing hours, including weekends. In the event Husband and Wife incur any type of tax due to the sale of the home, they shall equally share in the payment of that tax burden. Once the home closes, sales proceeds shall be assigned as follows:

Wife shall receive the first $65,000.00

Husband shall receive the second $65,000.00

Husband shall be reimbursed any principal (not interest) that he has paid down between the time Husband and Wife signed their separation agreement and the home closes sale.

Remaining proceeds shall be shared equally.

In the event Husband elects to accept an offer that does not yield at least $65,000.00 in net sale proceeds, Wife shall receive 100% of the net sale proceeds and Dave shall tender a payment to Wife in an amount equal to the difference in the proceeds she received and $65,000.00. Said payment shall be made within 7 days of the home closing sale and the proceeds being distributed.

Husband shall occupy the home until sold and Wife shall vacate the residence with all of her jointly agreed belongings on or before March 31, 2015. All moving costs that Wife incurs at the time she vacates the home shall be paid 100% by Wife, without contribution from Husband. Husband shall not rent the marital home or any portion thereof or obtain a roommate in order to prolong the sale of the home to any person as long as the deed is in both Husband and Wife's names. Husband shall claim the mortgage interest and real estate taxes relating to the marital home on any individual tax return he files.

In the event that Husband desires to refinance the home in the joint names of the parties in order to lower his monthly mortgage payment, he may do so as long as he pays 100% of any costs he may incur in obtaining said refinancing and the total amount of the principal balance of said refinanced mortgage does not exceed the total sum of the principal balances of the present two mortgages combined at the time of the refinance. If the terms and conditions of this paragraph are met by Husband, Wife shall co-operate by signing all required documents incident to said refinancing.

The parties agree that in the event Husband desires to refinance the mortgages into his sole name at any time prior to the home being sold, Wife shall sign any required documents to facilitate this refinance, as well as a Non-Warranty Deed transferring her right title and interest in said home to Husband upon her receiving said $65,000.00.

In the event that the sale of the home results in a deficiency at sale closing, Husband shall pay 100% of said deficiency at sale closing and within 7 days thereafter, Husband shall pay Wife the sum of $65,000.00 in full and complete satisfaction of her interest in the home.

The payments that Husband shall pay Wife pursuant to the terms and conditions of this paragraph are by way of property equalization, and not spousal support. In any event, Husband shall indemnify, save and hold Wife harmless from the payment of any obligations relating to any present or future debts associated with this home. The parties agree and acknowledge the risks associated with liability for a joint loan in the event the responsible party fails to abide by the terms of such loan.

Evaluation: This clause is suspect. No clause should have this many stipulations. Make efforts to understand the intent and make a clear and concise clause. Ideally, a real estate agent should be retained by both parties. A clause should be included that if any actions were taken to deliberately impede (be clear on this) the sale of this home by either party that the defaulting party shall indemnify and hold the other party harmless by paying for said (outline expenses to be reimbursed) expenses. The refinancing terms seem suspicious as well. There is obviously more to this situation than is presented.

Notes/questions for your attorney:

_____

_____

_____

_____

_____

Vehicles: All vehicles should be valued and any related liabilities should be identified. If vehicles are paid in full, the title to the vehicle should be signed over to the party retaining the vehicle. Efforts should be made to transfer the title and any outstanding liability into each party's name prior to signing the divorce agreement. The value of the vehicles can be easily attained free of charge by looking up the Kelley Blue Book® values at www.kbb.com.

Personal Priorities:

- Having a car that is appropriate for lifestyle, transporting children, specialized for work, and is reasonable for maintenance and repairs
- Having a car suitable for health needs and regular transportation and is economically efficient
- Having a car fully paid for and ensuring title is transferred
- Determining who is responsible for any related loans, maintenance, insurance and taxes
- Ensure liability is transferred to appropriate party

Items to Consider:

- It is important to consider the age and mileage of your vehicle and the cost to maintain the vehicle. For example, a couple with middle-school-aged children may want to consider that these children will be drivers themselves in the near future and will be borrowing or getting their own car for activities. A SUV may no longer be appropriate.

- A sports car is a wonderful second car, but not necessarily appropriate for all activities.
- Your car may be paid off, but if it has significant mileage, the future costs to maintain this vehicle will be disruptive and costly.
- If you are a spouse that has never maintained a vehicle, you will need to get familiar with all related costs for your vehicle: insurance, gas mileage, related taxes and fees, warranties and estimated costs of repairs and maintenance. These expenses will provide support for the amounts listed on your financial budget/affidavit.

Based on a true story – A couple had separated, and in their agreement, one party was to retain a Chevrolet van that was fully paid off. After several months, it was decided that it would be sensible to purchase a smaller, more economical vehicle. Upon purchase, the party was unable to trade in the vehicle because both parties still remained on the title of the vehicle. This situation was more stressful than it should have been.

Example 1 Sample Clause:

Wife operates a 2005 Volvo XC90, which is titled in the wife's name and is unencumbered. Simultaneously with the execution of this agreement, Husband shall transfer and convey too Wife all of his right, title and interest in and to said vehicle, and the same hereinafter be the sole and separate property of Wife. Wife shall be responsible for and discharge all obligations in connection with the ownership and operation of said vehicle, and she shall hold Husband harmless as a result.

Husband operates a Chevrolet Impala, which is a company car provided through his employment.

Evaluation: In this case, the division of assets is very straightforward. Based on the situation of the Wife, she may want to consider the age of the vehicle and the costs to maintain this vehicle. It may be appropriate to request a new vehicle be purchased in Wife's name before the divorce is final so that Wife is able to qualify and be approved for this purchase.

Example 2 Sample Clause:

There is a 2007 Ford truck titled in Steve's name with an agreed value of $18,575. The loan (Ally #xxx) is in Steve's name and has an outstanding balance of $5,524.00. Steve shall keep this vehicle and shall be responsible for the payments, insurance, tag, taxes, and other operating costs.

There is a 2006 Chevy Suburban titled in Steve and Donna's name with an agreed value of $21,300.00. It has been agreed that Donna will trade in this vehicle and purchase a new vehicle. Steve will sign all necessary paperwork to release title.

Evaluation: Donna should purchase a new vehicle prior to signing the divorce agreement to ensure she is easily able to acquire and finance a new vehicle. This also protects Donna in the event that a purchase is not approved and will allow Donna to renegotiate the terms of this clause.

Notes/questions for your attorney:

_____

_____

_____

_____

_____

Other Personal Property: Personal property includes personal belongings, furniture and fixtures, paintings, household items, recreational equipment and vehicles: wave-runners, boats, golf carts, trailers, lawn mowers, tools, household items, etc. It is most cost effective for the parties to come to an agreement on how these items will be allocated **_on their own_** and share this information with their attorneys to ensure allocations have been properly addressed. It is highly recommended that the separation of items take place before the divorce agreement is signed to ensure that there has not been any miscommunication on the allocation verbally discussed and agreed to. In the event that there is an issue, it should be resolved between the parties before an agreement is signed. In most instances, the cost to have "your way" far exceeds the value of the item.

Personal Priorities:

- In many cases, this is where the parties can become vindictive. Try to avoid this, as it will only cost you more money to deliberate over these items and personal angst.
- If you have already separated, than most items have already been allocated.

Items to Consider:

- In most instances, the cost to have "your way" far exceeds the value of the item.

Inherited Personal Property or Gifts: Any property received as a gift or inheritance is considered separate property, even if received during the marriage, if it is kept in a separate account. Personal gifts, such as jewelry and clothes, are usually always deemed separate property. A gift of a painting may be considered marital property if given to the couple. Unfortunately, if any monetary gifts received are deposited in a joint account or used for the purchase of a marital asset, these items are considered marital assets. That is why prenuptial agreements are made to protect the value of an estate if subsequently used as a marital asset. For example, if either party's family gives the couple a substantial gift towards purchasing a marital asset, it may be appropriate to have this asset listed in a prenuptial agreement. Alternatively, if one party owns a home prior to the marriage, if there is no prenuptial agreement, then this asset becomes marital property upon marriage.

Personal Priorities:

- Each party would like to ensure that gifts or inherited property remains with the party whose family gave the asset.
- The value of a collection should be valued, and alternative assets should be given to account for any disparity in the value of assets to be allocated.
- Tools used for business interests should be retained by the spouse with knowledge of their use.
- Recreational vehicles should be valued and or sold to provide equitable distribution. If one party chooses to keep any of these assets, a value should be assigned and reimbursed to the other party.

Items to Consider:

In most cases, the costs to engage an attorney to draft an agreement or allocation of personal items far exceeds the value of these items. It is customary for each individual to retain all his/her personal property, including gifts, jewelry and other personal items. While the value of some items, such as tools, guns and other collectibles, may be of significance, each party should draft his/her own list and allocation thereof.

If one party is unable to maintain, transport or house any asset of significance, a value should be assigned and reimbursed to the other party. <u>While we realize that allocation of these items can cause resentment for your change in lifestyle, it is important to look forward and consider your ability to use and maintain these assets.</u>

Because the allocation of personal property can be emotional and a means to be retaliatory, we strongly advise that you remain objective and impartial. The value of used tools, furniture and other household items is usually a lot less than most think they can be sold for. In addition, the time and effort it would take to liquidate these items would only cause further chaos. Again, try to separate personal property amongst yourselves without the costly involvement of professionals.

Based on a true story – A wife received an inheritance of $100,000, and she used this amount as a down payment to purchase the marital home. After five years of marriage, the couple decided to get a divorce. The wife requested that she receive the total value of her inheritance. The husband legally did not have to reimburse the wife his portion of the equity ($50,000). While she did not receive the entire amount of her inheritance, she mediated a settlement of $70,000.

While many couples never expect to get divorced or that their spouse would keep/request any of these amounts/items, the fact that 1 out of 2 marriages fail should encourage you to protect yourself in the future.

Example 1 Sample Clause:

Each of the parties hereto is to have his or her own individual property, such as clothing, jewelry, toilet articles and any and all personal property presently located in his or her possession.

Evaluation: This clause demonstrates how the parties proactively separated their assets prior to signing their agreement to avoid any unnecessary time and expense related to these items.

Example 2 Sample Clause:

The parties have agreed to the division of all of their general personal property and household contents between them, including, but not limited to all of their personal clothing, jewelry, sporting equipment, furniture and fixtures. All of the said items of general personal property which are in their individual possession as of the date they sign this Agreement are awarded to each of them as their sole and separate property. Any additional personal property items that have not been divided between the parties at the time that they sign this Agreement shall be divided between them whenever it is convenient to do so. It is anticipated by the parties that Wife will have items of personal property that will be located at the marital residence at the time the parties sign this Agreement and possibly after she moves from the marital residence. The parties declare that they do not require a detailed list of yet undivided personal property. They are confident that they will be able to complete their division of said property without difficulty. If any dispute occurs, they have agreed to return to mediation in order to resolve their differences before entering into litigation.

Evaluation: This is an example of an overly optimistic clause. Every clause should be clear and concise. In the event that certain actions cannot be completed prior to signing of the divorce agreement, measures should be taken to avoid further controversy. For example, if the above agreed upon items cannot be moved, the items should be clearly marked, packaged and sealed and listed in the divorce agreement to avoid additional expenses. It is recommended that all division of property should be done prior to signing of Divorce agreement whenever possible. Many individuals who are slighted or unhappy by the outcome of their agreement use this as an opportunity to aggravate the other party. In addition, the stipulation that if a dispute occurs, the couple will return to mediation to resolve their differences should be avoided. This clause should be clear the first time in order to avoid any additional expenses.

Notes/questions for your attorney:

_____

_____

_____

_____

_____

Investments and Bank Accounts: A complete list of all bank accounts and investments should be prepared as of the date of separation (or other date as advised by your attorney based on individual circumstances) with balances, cost basis and ownership details. All accounts should be reviewed prior to the date of separation to ensure that there were no large transactions or transfers made that would represent extraordinary expenses or misuse of funds for one's own personal benefit. Usually, one party is aware that he/she wants a divorce and begins to plan accordingly.

Each party is requested to prepare a financial budget/affidavit of their income and expenses as well as a listing of their assets and liabilities. If you do not know the details of your financial situation, your attorney can assist you in obtaining the necessary documentation.

Personal Priorities:

- Having enough cash to pay for an attorney and/or reasonable and customary living expenses
- Having access to cash during the divorce process when accounts are in one party's name or funds have been transferred to another account and are no longer accessible
- Obtaining the necessary knowledge to manage assets received, separate assets and plan for most efficient liquidation thereof

Items to Consider:

Unfortunately, one party may hoard or try to spend money so the other party will not be able have access or ability to recoup monies hidden or spent. Joint accounts are accessible by both parties. Either party is able to transfer monies to a separate account in his/her name only. If this is the case and one party is forced to use a credit card for customary and reasonable expenses, these amounts should be documented and shared with his/her attorney.

Upon review of the cash transactions for the past few years (or a timeframe that is considered reasonable), there may be large expenses or withdrawals that should be documented and for which explanations should be obtained. We have had countless cases where monies were used to purchase gifts for a partner outside the marriage or monies were transferred or given to a family member or friends. Extraordinary expenses that are above and beyond your family's customary living expenses should be documented for your attorney. Based on your personal situation and the advice of your attorney, if there is reason to believe that a spouse has hidden or misused funds, it would be appropriate to engage the services of a CDFA to assist with identification and options to allocate marital assets.

It is also extremely important to consider the cost basis when comparing assets for allocation along with any other costs that may be incurred for the separation and or liquidation of those assets.

Based on a true story - *Janet and Jake are getting divorced and they are both age 64. They had two assets: an investment account worth $180,000 and a money market account worth $180,000. Janet was really concerned about retirement and wanted to take the retirement fund. It felt more secure to her. After the divorce was final, they each wanted to buy a small house. Jake took $90,000 for a down payment out of his money market fund to make the down payment on his house. Janet asked for $90,000 from the investment account to make a down payment on her house but the net amount she realized was only $60,000 due to the taxes she owed on money from the investment account! Remember that you cannot compare a cash account with an investment account without knowing the cost basis of those investments and the related tax consequences.*

Based on a true story – *A man from India, married and working in the United States, met another woman on a business trip when traveling to India. He began a relationship with this woman and began to transfer monies to India and to purchase gifts for several years. He wanted to remain in America for his job and until his daughter went to college. The wife began to accumulate financial records to try to quantify the amounts spent so that she could be equitably be reimbursed from other assets. Lucky for her, there were enough assets remaining to reimburse and distribute the marital assets equitably.*

Example 1 Sample Clause:

Husband is the owner of a brokerage account with Prudential, which had approximate securities, cash and margin composition as follows:

Bank of America	100	shares
Precious Metals Holdings	145.5	shares
Vanguard All Cap Value Fund	1234	shares
Goldstein Balanced Fund	1576	shares

Margin Balance	$28,854.56

Wife shall be entitled to receive one-half of the total cash and securities of said account held in Husband's name as of the date of separation.

Husband is the owner of a Money Market account with Prudential. Simultaneously with the execution of this Agreement, said account shall become the sole and separate property of Husband. Wife shall be entitled to receive $23,000 of the total cash value of said account.

The parties shall immediately close any joint bank accounts and split the balance as of the date of separation of said accounts equally.

Evaluation: Again, very clear and concise. There is an inherent risk when a specific date is given. The actual distribution date of the monies can happen at a much later date. The investment may have increased or decreased.

Example 2 Sample Clause:

Husband is awarded the following investment accounts, which include all present and future deposits in said accounts. The balances disclosed in the Agreement were approximate balances at the time the parties mediated their Agreement. These accounts are held in Bryan's sole name.

Merrill Lynch- 6447	$15,000.00
Fidelity – 83368	$ 6,780.00
Fidelity – 79905	$ 5,654.00

The following banking accounts are jointly held and are used to meet the parties' marital expenses on a month-to-month basis. Effective as of the date of the parties' physical separation, Husband is awarded the remaining balance of each account. Within 30 days following the signing of their separation agreement, the parties shall attempt to have Wife's name removed as a responsible party to each account. If her name cannot be removed, the respective account shall be immediately closed and all funds on deposit at that time shall be paid to Husband.

Sun Trust - 0966876
Bank of America – 7744543
Bank of America - 5563289

Evaluation: This clause is very clear.

Notes/questions for your attorney:

_____

_____

_____

_____

_____

Line of Credit: A line of credit is a loan that is usually collateralized by the excess equity in your home. During the divorce process, we have found that many couples that are strapped for cash use monies from their line of credit to pay for various expenses. Discuss options with your attorney to ensure that funds should not be released unless approved by both parties.

Personal Priorities:

- Having cash to retain an attorney and pay related divorce expenses until a divorce agreement is signed
- Having cash to meet living expenses

Items to Consider:

Parties have taken advantage by withdrawing monies from their line of credit for their own personal use. The said liability is then deducted from the proceeds of the home when it is sold. This can generate some interesting discussions on how allocations of other marital assets could be made. If one party has taken money from the line of credit without mutual consent, make sure you document all withdrawals.

Notes/questions for your attorney:

_____

_____

_____

_____

_____

Unsecured Debt – Credit Cards: A credit report should be run on each party to ascertain any outstanding liabilities. Whenever possible, it is recommended that all debt be paid in full and all joint credit cards are closed before the divorce agreement is signed. Each party should obtain a credit card in his/her own name based on his/her separate income. Debt incurred prior to separation or divorce is still the liability of both parties, no matter whose name is on the application. Credit was approved based on the information on the application as a married person and total household income; therefore, both parties are liable for the debt. All unsecured debt should be identified in the divorce agreement with details noting which accounts will be closed and paid off. For any outstanding balances, arrangements should be made to close the account and details documenting how the remaining balance will be paid. We highly encourage you to discuss viable options with your attorney to ensure you are protecting your personal interests.

Personal Priorities:

- Being able to make purchases if credit cards have been closed or one party is no longer an authorized user

- Having access to cash during the divorce process when credit cards are in one party's name
- The ability to have a credit card in one party's name
- The payment of related debts when parties separate

Items to Consider:

If one party does not have a credit card in his/her name alone, it is recommended that he/she apply for one in his/her name only. This will enable that party to begin to create credit for himself/herself. Before the divorce agreement is signed, all joint credit card liabilities should be paid off, and accounts should be closed and reopened in one party's name.

Based on a true story – *In order to save money, a couple decided to remain living together until they could come to an agreement on the allocation and distribution of their assets. The husband paid all expenses and gave the wife a sizable allowance while they were still living together. Near the end of their settlement it was discovered that the wife ran up $25,000 in credit card debt over the past four months. The husband was extremely angry, and their property settlement became extremely contentious and the wife finally agreed to manage 70% of the related debt.*

Example 1 Sample Clause:

Each party shall be solely responsible for any and all debt in his or her sole name, and hold the other harmless as a result thereof. The parties stipulate that no further charges shall be caused to any existing joint accounts and that all such accounts shall be immediately closed.

Neither party shall charge or cause to be charged to or against the other party any debt nor secure any credit upon or in connection with the other or in the name of the other, and each party shall promptly pay all debts and discharge all financial obligations which he or she may incur or may have incurred since the separation of the parties and shall indemnify, save and hold harmless the other from such debts and financial obligations.

Evaluation: This clause is clear and provides recourse if parties do not comply.

Example 2 Sample Clause:

Husband is awarded the following debts as his sole and separate debts. Husband shall indemnify, save and hold Wife harmless from the payment of any of said debts:

The following individual credit card accounts which are held in his sole name are assigned to Husband as his sole and separate obligations:

Bank of America – signature loan	$2,750.00
American Express – Bank of America	$ -
Belk – GEMB	$ -
MasterCard – Citi	$ -

Wife is awarded the following debts as her sole and separate debts. Wife shall indemnify, save and hold Husband harmless from the payment of any of said debts:

The following individual credit card accounts which are held in her sole name are assigned to Wife as her sole and separate obligations:

Visa – Bank of America	$ -
Jcrew – WFNNB	$ -
Sears	$1,236.88
Ann Taylor	$ -
Mastercard – Capital One	$2,654.53

Evaluation: While the agreement assigns responsibility of these obligations, all of these debts were secured with cards that were approved with joint income amounts. In the event that there is an issue, the credit card company has the right to pursue both parties since the debt was incurred while married. It would be in the Husband's best interest to ensure all outstanding debt is paid and accounts are closed. If there is any outstanding balances, they should be transferred to a new card in the responsible party's sole name.

Notes/questions for your attorney:

_____

_____

_____

_____

_____

Other Investments/Business Interests:

Other investments/business interests include items, such as but not limited to, stock options issued but not exercised, personal business ventures or annuities, rental properties, etc. Many couples have assets and income related to their own personal businesses and extraordinary investments. The financial information related to these assets can be found by analyzing tax returns: Schedule C, pay stubs, employee investment statements, and/or corporate or partnership returns. If any of these assets is deemed to be of significant value, it would be in your best interest to have a professional third party value these assets.

There are many aspects to be considered when separating personal investment and business assets. Your Property Settlement Agreement should stipulate how these interests will be divided and managed in the future. If there are any related liabilities, ensure that this debt is legally transferred into the correct party's name and/or that of the business interest.

Personal Priorities:

- Am I getting a fair settlement or distribution from these assets?
- Am I entitled to future income?
- What are the tax implications to each party upon transfer and liquidation?

- Who is instrumental to the longevity and existence of the company?
- What do I do with these assets?

Items to Consider:

There are many items to consider, plan for and manage related to these assets. Ensuring that a proper valuation is determined and an understanding of all related costs and future tax considerations is imperative when these assets are being divided and/or received. It is highly recommended that you consult with a qualified CDFA to review your options.

Based on true story – *The couple had the residential home (valued at $460,000 purchased for $250,000 with a remaining mortgage of $160,000) and an investment property worth $325,000 (tax basis was $135,000).*

The husband wanted to keep the house valued at $300,000 net of mortgage balance and the wife was to receive the investment property valued at $325,000. The reality of this is that the investment property is worth only $265,000 net of capital gains taxes and closing costs. This is why it is important to understand the retail value and well as the liquidation value of an asset.

Stock Options: While Section 1041 of the tax code provides that no gain or loss is recognized on a transfer of property between spouses and former spouses if the transfer is incident to divorce, stock options have different rules. These assets can be very tricky and should be valued according to their ability to provide income, transferability and tax consequences to each party when exercised. Consult a professional to ensure you have the ability to accomplish what is intended when trying to value and allocate these assets.

Based on a true story – *A couple had divorced and as a part of the settlement. the husband was awarded stock options from his company. When the husband left the company and exercised the options, he had to pay a* *significant amount of taxes. The valuation at the time of the divorce did not take into account these additional expenses.*

Separating or determining a value for a business owned by either party: *It can be very stressful when determining the value of a business, managerial roles and viability of future income streams. <u>Consult a professional to ensure you have the ability to accomplish what is intended when trying to value and allocate these assets.</u>*

Notes/questions for your attorney:

_____

_____

_____

_____

_____

Life Insurance – Since alimony/spousal support payments usually terminate upon the death of the payor and/or can be reduced if the payor becomes disabled, each party should consider having a life insurance policy or a term policy as deemed necessary based on the couple's circumstances. Life insurance is usually purchased to protect against loss of income for the payment of alimony and/or child support.

Personal Priorities:

- Do I have protection for future payments if my former spouse dies or becomes disabled?
- Is there life insurance provided or purchased through my former spouse's company?
- Can there be an irrevocable beneficiary assignment?
- Is a separate policy needed?

Items to Consider:

It is best to have the beneficiary of the policy also be the owner of the policy. This will ensure that the premiums are being paid timely and that there will be no unauthorized changes to the designated beneficiary. The ages and circumstances of the couple's situation will determine the priority of having life insurance.

Example 1 Sample Clause:

Husband shall maintain a life insurance policy on both Husband's and Wife's life for the benefit and care of the minor children, XXX and XXXX. Husband will be the sole and separate owner of all Life Insurance policies. Wife waives, renounces, and relinquishes any and all interest she may have in said policies.

Except as set forth herein, each party stipulates that each will be the sole and separate owner of any and all Life Insurance in his or her sole name, and each party waives, renounces and relinquishes any and all interest he or she may have in the Life Insurance in the name of the other party.

Evaluation: This clause does not discuss the beneficiary assignments, nor does it provide the Wife assurances that the policies will be maintained. The agreement should also state the policy numbers and type of policy purchased. Depending on the type of policy purchased, term or whole life, there may be other items to consider. Typically, life insurance is on the life of the primary income provider.

Example 2 Sample Clause:

Husband shall carry a life insurance policy or group policies with an aggregate benefit of $1,000,000.00 on himself until July 30, 2018. The primary beneficiary of this level of death benefit shall be Wife. In the event Wife requests evidence of insurance that demonstrates Husband's compliance with this provision, Husband shall provide such evidence within 14 days of the request. Husband may name any secondary beneficiaries of his choosing.

Wife shall carry a life insurance policy or group policies with an aggregate benefit of $1,000,000.00 on herself until July 30, 2018. The primary beneficiary of this level of death benefit shall be Husband. In the event Husband requests evidence of insurance that demonstrates Husband's compliance with this provision, Wife shall provide such evidence within 14 days of the request. Wife may name any secondary beneficiaries of his choosing.

Evaluation: In order to avoid any further communication or to ensure that the said policies are being maintained, each beneficiary should be the owner of the policy from which they would benefit. Again, the dollar amount of the policies should be in align with the circumstances of each couple. It is not clear why the Wife would have to maintain such a large policy on herself.

Notes/questions for your attorney:

_____

_____

_____

_____

_____

Retirement Plans and Income: Retirement assets along with the marital home are usually couples most significant assets. It is extremely important to understand the nature of retirement assets held. There are many nuances based upon the retirement plan document for each plan, and these details can have a direct impact on the future cash flow available to each party. Generally, there are four types of potential retirement income: Defined Contribution Plans, Defined Benefit Plans, Individual Retirement Accounts (IRAs), and Social Security. Each of these retirement accounts have very specific considerations to ensure proper allocation, avoidance of tax payments or penalties and timing concerns that will offer maximum benefits. It is highly recommended that you consult with a CDFA and a divorce financial planner to ensure you understand what the values are of each asset and the best manner to structure receipt of these benefits to maximize the related benefits for each party. It is in the best interest of both parties to understand their retirement benefits. In many cases, the allocation of these assets can make both parties future cash flow more beneficial and sometimes reduce the amount of alimony to be paid. Defined Contribution and Defined Pension plans both require the use of a QDRO to allocate benefits. A QDRO is an order from the court to the retirement plan administrator with detailed instructions to clarify and document the benefits that will be divided between parties in a divorce. It is in the best interest of the parties to begin the preparation of the QDRO to ensure there will be no complications after the divorce agreement is complete. This document outlines the benefits of the pension plan allocation to the parties in alignment with the pension plan documents provisions. Unfortunately, most QDROs are unable to be completed in entirety until after the divorce agreement has been signed. The QDRO must be approved by the plan administrator to be effective and enforceable. <u>Do not finalize your agreement if there is any indication that the QDRO will not be completed and accepted as intended.</u>

<u>Defined Contribution Plans</u> are most commonly recognized as 401(k) plans whereby the employee makes contributions and the employer may offer matching contributions based upon the plan document. It is very easy to determine the value of a 401(k) as statements are issued on a regular basis. By reviewing the statements, one can determine if there have been any loans or withdrawals. Based on the timing of the loans and withdrawals made, there may be arguments whether these withdrawals should be added back to the asset value for consideration in the final separation and allocation of assets. The marital portion of these assets is determined based on the length of time of the marriage divided by the length of time of participation in the plan. This percentage is then applied to the balance of the account. If there is a vesting schedule associated with the plan, then the account value would be determined based on the earned vested amount and the marital percentage would then be applied to that balance.

A distribution from a retirement account made prior to age 59 ½ is considered an early distribution and is subject to a 10% penalty.

The Internal Revenue Service Code Section (72)(t)(2)(C) provides an exception to the 10% penalty when withdrawn from a qualified plan by an ex-spouse in accordance with a written QDRO.

> **Please note: The distribution allowed is limited to the benefits provided for under the plan. In addition, a distribution from a qualified plan is subject to 20% federal income tax withholding by the plan unless made directly to an IRA and you will have to pay taxes on the distribution if you receive monies directly.**

Items to Consider:

There are many crucial items that need to be addressed when preparing a QDRO. It is imperative that this order is prepared timely and approved by the plan administrator prior to signing the divorce agreement. After you are divorced, it will be extremely difficult and costly to make adjustments and/or corrections.

No matter what your divorce agreement states, the pension plan document legally overrides anything that the parties agree to. The pension plan document has specific details about the allocation of funds, survivor benefits (if any) and valuation thereof.

Many governmental plans are very strict and only allow one attempt at getting a QDRO approved. Ensure you are working with an experienced professional when attempting to get your QDRO approved.

Defined Benefit Plans are generally referred to as pensions. These assets are benefits given by an employer to its employee based on years of service and amount of salary received. The amount of benefit cannot be readily determined. It is in the best interest of the non-employee spouse to have the marital portion of this asset calculated by a professional. Do not rely on the amounts given by your spouse, an accountant or any other person who does not make these calculations on a routine basis. Ask your attorney for a recommendation or reach out to a Collaborative Law Group association in your area for a list of reputable, experienced and professional CDFAs or divorce financial planners who can serve you. Many private companies have phased out these types of retirement benefits, but many governmental agencies still have this type of retirement benefit. Be patient, as it may take time to gather all the necessary information to make an accurate assessment of this retirement asset. In most cases, it is well worth the wait. <u>A distribution from these types of plans is also done through the issuance of a QDRO.</u>

Please note: <u>Some of these types of plans (ie. public employee pensions) are not transferable to an ex-spouse per the plan document. Read the plan documents benefits carefully.</u>

THE PLAN DOCUMENT SUPERSEDES ANY REQUEST OR LANGUAGE IN A DIVORCE AGREEMENT. Ensure you have a complete and accurate understanding of the benefits allowed and allocations thereof. The QDRO must be approved by the plan administrator to be effective and enforceable. It is recommended that the QDRO be approved before your plan document is signed to avoid any misunderstandings.

<u>**IRAs**</u> are investments made by either party for their own retirement and are in their own name. These balances are considered marital property if they were set up and accumulated during the marriage. If the accounts were owned prior to the marriage, only the subsequent contributions and earnings would be considered marital assets. Since IRAs are not considered qualified plans, a QDRO is not needed.

Please note: You should check with the trustee of the IRA to ascertain what type of documentation is needed to distribute, transfer or divide the IRA. In most cases, the trustee will only need a copy of the divorce or property settlement agreement. This distribution is not subject to the 20% withholding. In order to avoid the 10% early-withdrawal penalty if you are younger than 59 ½, you can take equal periodic distributions for a period of 5 years or until you are 59 ½ years of age.

<u>**Social Security Benefits**</u>: As an individual you are entitled to Social Security benefits based on your income and/or the benefits of **ANY** spouse you were married to for 10 years or more. You can elect to receive social security retirement benefits as early as age 59 1/2. Full retirement benefits vary based on the age of an individual and that of the wage-earner spouse. Please consult with a Social Security Administration (SSA) representative to ensure the details of eligibility for your retirement benefits and that of your former spouse. This will enable you to evaluate which benefits will be most beneficial to you.

Personal Priorities:
- Are there concerns that there is adequate income available to retire?
- Are you aware of how to obtain information related to your benefits or that of your spouse?
- How do I manage my benefits and social security?
- When is the best time to begin taking payments?
- My spouse is older than I am; when can I start receiving benefits?
- My spouse is younger than I am; when can I start receiving benefits?

Items to Consider:
When trying to determine the value of the retirement assets, it is highly recommended that an experienced professional be consulted. It is easiest to weigh your options for your personal needs by looking at a cash flow projection of income.

If there is a significant illness that would cause an extreme financial burden, then we would advise you to <u>ask your attorney about the benefits of having a Legal Separation Agreement that becomes a formal divorce agreement and is filed on a designated future date.</u> This option would allow for the existing medical coverage to remain intact and increase cash flow to both parties until other arrangements could be made. This example is meant for older couples awaiting social security and Medicare benefits or when there are significant health considerations.

Based on a true story – A woman was 4 years younger than her spouse and had very serious health condition and costs. It was recommended that the couple remain married until the woman could begin Medicaid and receive social security. This provided benefits to the woman and reduced the current and future amounts of alimony payments to be made by her spouse.

<u>Example 1 Sample Clause:</u>

Husband is the owner of a 401(k) account through his employment with Duke Power, which had an approximate share balance as of date of separation of 9,678.980 shares. Wife shall be entitled to receive one-half of the total shares of said account as of date of separation.

Husband is owner of a pension account through his employment with Duke Power. Husband and Wife agree that Husband shall be the sole and separate owner of said pension account and Wife hereby waives, renounces, and relinquishes any and all interest she may have in said account.

Except as provided hereinabove, Husband and Wife shall each be the sole and separate owner of his or her own individual retirement plans each may have via his or her employment.

Evaluation: The wife relinquished her share or rights in the Husband's pension account through his employment. The Wife may have overlooked a very significant future asset. The amount appears to be significant based on the Husband salary, number of years of employment and other general information.

Example 2 Sample Clause:

Husband is awarded the following retirement accounts, which include all present and future deposits in said accounts. The balances disclosed in the Agreement were approximate balances at the time the parties mediated their agreement. These accounts are held in Husband's sole name.

Fidelity – Pension Restoration plan	$ 3,049.00
Fidelity 401k	$ 74,444.00
Fidelity Defined Contribution	$110,958.00

Wife shall promptly sign spousal death benefit waivers for any of the above accounts that require a waiver (before Dave would be able to change the beneficiaries named on the accounts) any time that Dave presents the waivers to her for her signature.

Evaluation: The last sentence is confusing but is intended to ensure that in the event that the Husband dies before the couple's divorce becomes final (one year of separation required in their state), that he will be able to change the designated beneficiaries to someone other than his spouse.

Notes/questions for your attorney:

_____

_____

_____

_____

_____

Summary:

When allocating assets, it is more cost efficient to assign each asset in aggregate to each party rather than separating the total value 50/50. To adjust the allocation of marital assets, it is easiest to make adjustments to the equity allocation from the sale of the marital home or allocation determined for the division of retirement assets. It is highly recommended that a CDFA be engaged to ascertain accurate valuation of assets and prepare cash flow projections to allow you to make better decisions for your future.

<u>Review the following checklist before you sign off on your Property Settlement Agreement:</u>

- If the marital home is sold or transferred to one party, ensure that you have received a document from the mortgage company releasing you from any liabilities.
- Ensure that the deed of the home is properly transferred and recorded.
- Section 1041 of the IRS tax code has guidelines that allow tax-free transfer of property if it is incident to divorce. <u>Ensure that you are aware of the cost basis of any assets received and improvements made thereto</u>. This cost basis will be used for calculation of any gain or loss when sold. Ensure that each party is aware of the tax implications or possible recapture requirements. Understanding them is important because the spouse who receives the property in the transfer assumes all the tax attributes of the spouse who transferred the property, including the need to recapture prior tax benefits. This means that receiving spouse bears the tax impact of the recapture provisions upon a subsequent sale, exchange or other taxable disposition of the property. (Examples include rental property and any assets used in a business that was previously depreciated.)
- Ensure that all vehicle titles have been transferred and any related liabilities refinanced.
- Ensure that all credit card debt has been paid or that any remaining debt is transferred to a separate account in the name of responsible party. If there are any concerns, credit reports should be run on each party.

- Ensure that all assets have been accounted for and that you are aware of the tax basis of any asset received and the tax implications if that asset is sold at a future date. If there are any concerns that all financial information has been received, consult with your attorney.

- If you own your own business, there are valuation considerations, assignment of managerial duties if both parties were engaged in the operations thereof and things to consider to ensure future streams of income to both parties if necessary.

- Engage a CFDA/CPA to properly value and communicate the tax implications of dividing stock options and other investments.

- Review the need for life insurance.

- Engage a CFDA or professional third party to prepare and calculate the value of any retirement accounts.

- Engage an experienced professional to prepare a QDRO for the release and assignment of your retirement benefits. (Ideally this process should be done immediately to ensure segregation of assets can be completed as intended.) <u>If the pension is a governmental pension, it is strongly suggested that you consult with a QDRO specialist, as there are rules that may disqualify future benefits if not prepared accurately the *first* time.</u>

- Set up an account with the SSA so that you will have access to your benefits and any changes thereto. It is recommended that you set up a meeting with the SSA a year prior to receiving your benefits to ensure that all necessary documentation is completed to ensure you will be receiving timely benefit payments from the SSA.

- Retain copies of Social Security benefits for your former spouse and his/her social security number, date and place of birth and names of parents so you are prepared to consult with a SSA representative to track your retirement options.

- If you are the wage earner and are changing your name, make sure that you notify the SSA and your employer at the same time to ensure you will receive credit for all withholdings.
- Engage a CFDA/CPA to prepare cash flow projections and options based on the appreciating and depreciating assets you may receive to give you a conservative financial picture of future years. This analysis will give you piece of mind that you have made a fair settlement and will help you manage your life after the divorce is finalized.

Please Note: While the checklist above offers some suggestions to avoid future chaos, it is not inclusive of all the items that may be applicable to your personal situation. Please consult with your attorney.

CHAPTER 5
Spousal Support

Spousal Support:

In general, spousal support, alimony, and maintenance are terms used interchangeably to describe the monetary payment to be made by the supporting spouse to the dependent spouse, whose income is less or none at all. Check your state statutes for guidance on how alimony is determined. Some states have formulas that assist in the determination of spousal support and other states simply provide guidelines. The negotiation process can be very difficult when trying to quantify an appropriate and fair spousal support amount. For example, in NC, there are 16 factors that are considered when making an alimony determination. According to the North Carolina General Statutes section 50-16.3A, these 16 factors have been summarized as follows:

1. Any marital misconduct
2. The earnings and earning capacities of each spouse
3. The ages and physical, mental and emotional health/condition of each spouse
4. The amount and sources of earned and unearned income for each spouse (i.e., wages, dividends and earnings related to benefits such as medical, retirement, insurance and social security)
5. The number of years the parties were married

6. The contribution by one spouse to the education, training and/or increased earning potential of the other spouse
7. The extent to which the earning power of the dependent spouse will be affected by serving as custodian of a minor children
8. Standard of living of each spouse
9. The education of each of the spouses and time necessary to acquire sufficient education or training to enable the spouse to find employment that meets reasonable economic needs
10. The assets and liabilities of the spouses and debt service requirements of the spouses, including legal obligations of support
11. Any property brought to the marriage by either spouse
12. The contribution of a spouse as a homemaker
13. The needs of each spouse
14. Federal, state and local tax ramifications of the alimony reward
15. Any other factors relating to the economic circumstances of the parties that are considered just and proper
16. The fact that income was received by either party depending on the value of distributed marital assets

It is important to note in NC that if a spouse engages in "an act of illicit sexual behavior" (as defined in general statutes 50-16.1A(3)a.), during the marriage, on or before the date of separation by the dependent spouse, then no alimony is expected to be awarded; likewise if the supporting spouse engages in "an act of illicit sexual behavior" during the marriage, on or before the date of separation, he or she will automatically be responsible for payment of alimony considering all other relevant factors of the separation.

Each state has general statutes that provide information on the calculations and determining factors for spousal support.

> Determining the ***amount*** of spousal support
> to be paid is the million-dollar question and
> usually the first question that a dependent
> spouse will ask of an attorney.

As you can surmise at this point, this amount will probably be the last item to be resolved when preparing your divorce agreement. The determination of the amount of spousal support to be paid takes into account numerous factors (as noted above), and in NC there is no specific formula or calculation. This is where the use of a CDFA can be extremely advantageous in determining an amount that is reasonable and based on financial information provided by each party.

> A great starting point would be to have a calculation
> that provided an alimony amount based on a 50/50
> split of your income and child support based on a
> 50/50 shared custody arrangement. Based on your
> individual needs these percentages can be adjusted
> accordingly for negotiation purposes. See Appendix E.

It is in your best interest to begin thinking of a plan that will enable you to be self-sufficient and how you will get there. If age or illness is a factor, then proper presentation of your needs and circumstances will assist in this endeavor. The items discussed in Chapter 2 will also be beneficial in planning and preparing a logical and financial presentation of the dependent parties' needs. A CDFA will be able to take into consideration the needs and goals of each party and prepare options for consideration. A financial presentation based on the available income and each party's needs allows both individuals to digest his/her circumstance and help to manage personal expectations.

Personal Priorities:

There may be many concerns due to the age, education level and health of the dependent party and his/her ability to generate income to support themselves. Based on the age of the supporting spouse, there may be concerns over the ability to provide future income and plan for retirement. <u>The determination of spousal support is an extremely emotional and controversial topic between separating spouses.</u>

Items to Consider:

- Is rehabilitative support needed to re-enter the work force or to acquire skills that will allow for advancement and the ability to be self-supporting?
- The supporting spouse would like to pay as little support as possible for the least amount of time.
- The dependent spouse will need to separate her emotions and focus on the reality and possibilities of his/her position.
- What is the best allocation of assets compared to the amount of income available for alimony?
- Are there gaps between when alimony ends and retirement income is provided?
- Are there provisions in the agreement that provide protection in the event that the supporting spouse dies or becomes disabled?
- You are encouraged to consider **The Collaborative Law Divorce Process.**
- Ideas and options for consideration are much more well received when presented by a third party whose primary goal is to seek a fair and equitable resolution.
- Be open to options that will provide long-term benefits to yourself and your entire family.

We have provided you with the following sample alimony clauses for your review:

Example 1 Sample Clause:

Husband has agreed to pay Wife alimony in a sum equal to 25% of his gross per annum salary or other gross earnings from employment income not to include interest, dividends, or capital gains from invested assets. This shall be paid monthly on the 5th day of each month. Husband's annual income was $XXXXXX for the first year of employment and $XXXXXX for the second year of employment beginning October 5, 2016. Husband is currently employed by XXXXXXX. "Earned income" shall include bonuses or other distributions incident to his employment in recognition of his services. The parties have attached as Exhibits "B" and "C" to outline compensation terms with his place of employment, as well as his expenses and reimbursement schedule to lend clarity to the manner of his compensation. Husband agrees to utilize his best efforts to remain gainfully employed working on a "full time" schedule subject to any future limitations imposed by any health impediments. Alimony shall terminate upon the first to occur of the following terms and conditions:

a. Remarriage of Wife;
b. Cohabitation of Wife as defined in NCGS 50-16.9 (b);
c. Death of Husband;
d. Death of Wife;
e. Ceases upon attaining age 67.

For divorce agreements signed after 12/31/2018, alimony payments will no longer be deductible for the purposes of filing State and Federal income tax returns.

Evaluation:

This is a very clear and concise agreement describing the amounts to be paid. There may be other clauses to consider if there are concerns related to job stability, health issues or location of current or future jobs (may move overseas or another state). It would be preferable if payment is made via electronic transfer on date as outlined.

Example 2 Sample Clause:

Husband shall pay Wife spousal support in the amount of $XXXX per month for a period of 132 consecutive months for a total amount of $XXXXXX. Payments shall be due on the 20th day of each month by electronic funds transfer. Husband may, at his option, make two individual payments with 50% due on the 1th day of the month and the second payment due on the 15th of the month, with two months notice. The first installment shall take place on the date the parties sign this Agreement.

In the event that wife has more than $XXXX of taxable earned (employment related) income in any calendar year; spousal support shall be reduced by 50%.

Husbands financial obligation shall terminate whenever the first of the following events occur:

1. Wife's cohabitation with a person as defined by the North Carolina General Statutes in section 50-16.9(b)
2. The death of Wife
3. The remarriage of Wife
4. The death of Husband
5. Husband's last required payment as set forth hereinabove is paid.

The spousal support described in this section shall not be modifiable.

THE PROVISIONS FOR THE PAYMENT OF POST SEPARATION SUPPORT AND ALIMONY TO WIFE ARE INDEPENDENT OF ANY DIVISION OR AGREEMENT FOR DIVISION OF PROPERTY BETWEEN THE PARTIES, AND SHALL NOT FOR ANY PURPOSE BE DEEMED TO BE A PART OF OR MERGED

IN OR INTEGRATED WITH THE PROPERTY SETTLEMENT OF THE PARTIES AS SET FORTH IN THIS AGREEMENT.

Evaluation: While this clause is fairly inclusive it does have certain areas that should be more specific to avoid further chaos or discord. There should be a single definitive date for payment of spousal support and there should not be a reduction in the amount of support based on achievement of a set amount of salary by the supporting spouse (not recommended). This would only cause more stress and interruption of their future lives. And the last item that should be discussed with your attorney is the statement that this spousal support shall be modifiable or non-modifiable and what that would mean to you the spouse and the supporting spouse.

Notes/questions for your attorney:

_____

_____

_____

_____

_____

Related Clauses:
Documentation of Earnings:

Husband shall furnish to Wife reasonable documentation verifying his earned annual income (i.e. W-2's, 1099's, etc.) on an annual basis for each calendar year.

Evaluation: It is not typically recommended that this type of information need to be shared after the divorce is complete. Although, there are certain types of income that may warrant a creative approach.

Waiver of Other or Further Alimony:

Except as set forth hereinabove, Wife hereby expressly relinquishes and waives any and all rights to alimony or claims for maintenance and support from Husband. Husband hereby expressly relinquishes and waives any and all rights to alimony or claims for maintenance and support from Wife.

Evaluation: This statement is usually added when Alimony is considered non-modifiable.

Life Insurance to Secure Alimony:

So long as Husband has an alimony obligation to Wife, he shall keep in full force and effect his current term life insurance policy through xxxxxx company which has a death benefit of $xxxxxx. Wife shall be designated as the beneficiary of this policy until Husband's alimony obligation is satisfied in full.

Evaluation: This can be tricky as the employee usually has the right to change beneficiaries at any time. Over time this is very difficult to monitor and there have been cases where the policy was cancelled or there was a change in the beneficiary. If there is not enough income in the estate there is no recourse. The purpose and purchase of an insurance policy should be handled with care and all scenarios should be addressed as best as possible given the type of insurance, terms agreed to, beneficiary designations and modifications possible. In addition, depending on the type of insurance purchased, it may provide an investment benefit if not used. The allocation of the remaining proceeds should be addressed as well when the insurance is no longer required, specifically when the insurance is only required to secure alimony.

Summary:

It is apparent that the determination of spousal support is usually the most difficult part of the negotiation process for couples when separating. That is why it is usually the last item to be addressed in the negotiation process. **In many instances, there is little to no cash available to maintain two households in the manner to which each party was accustomed, especially when there are child support considerations.**

This is why it is extremely important to review your personal financial situation. A CDFA using a divorce family law software can easily provide multiple what-if scenarios that will help you manage your expectations. *See Appendix E.*

Understanding your financial limitations will enable you to plan accordingly. Many parties waste a great deal of time and money chasing unrealistic expectations. In many instances this information is not well received but enables clients to redirect their energy and develop ways to move forward that are feasible.

It is best to consider all aspects of the divorce agreement when determining the amount of spousal support: tax considerations (<u>Agreements entered into after December 31, 2018, alimony is no longer a deduction for tax purposes</u>), long–term benefits, asset allocations, cash flow needs, net worth projections and capital expenditures. There may be a better way to structure the allocation of assets that would provide a spousal support amount that would be most beneficial to BOTH parties). This is extremely important when there are children involved.

CHAPTER 6
Other Pertinent Agreements/ Disclosures

Other Pertinent Agreements/Disclosures: These are clauses that are intended for the protection of each party's interest and are intended to ensure that each party has provided accurate information so that a fair and equitable agreement can be reached. Each of these agreements/ disclosures has a very important and specific purpose. Please be sure to review these necessary disclosures with your attorney and ensure that you have a clear understanding of their purpose and their applicability to your situation.

In a Mediated Separation and Property Settlement Agreement, the following disclosure may be included:

The parties have also jointly engaged Attorney, XXXXX, a duly licensed North Carolina attorney, for the specific purpose of drafting this Mediated Separation and Property Settlement Agreement (Agreement) as a neutral who has the responsibility of setting forth the agreed upon terms and conditions of the parties Agreement in a form that would be legally enforceable pursuant to North Carolina law. The parties understand that Attorney XXXXX is acting solely in that Capacity; that he does not represent either party; that he will not give either party legal advice and he shall not advocate the individual interests of either party.

Both parties were advised of their right to seek independent counsel from an attorney-at-law, accountant, divorce financial planner, tax specialist, therapist, or other professional since this agreement affects substantial rights, obligations, and emotional situations of the parties and their children. *Any party who signs this Agreement without such counsel waives any issue or defense based on not having separate counsel.*

> **This agreement affects you and the welfare of your children for many years to come! Are you sure it is wise to enter into an agreement of this magnitude without professional assistance?**

Evaluation: Although, there is a Dispute Resolution Commission (Statute-7A-38.2) established under the Judicial Department that regulates standards for mediators and other neutrals, it is imperative that you understand that these parties are engaged to facilitate in the negotiation process but do not represent either party. It is up to you to thoroughly understand what you are agreeing to and its potential impact to your finances and general wellbeing.

BEWARE! There are many professionals that take advantage of this emotional transition. It is highly recommended that you have a Collaborative Law Attorney Mediator to ensure that he/she will be an advocate for a thorough and fair settlement agreement for both parties.

Based on a true story – A woman was in the midst of the mediation process when she began to panic and sought an attorney that would independently review her document and offer an opinion and/or suggestions. She was told in her consultation that she would need to provide a retainer of $5,000 and *any unused funds would be returned to her as the woman was unsure of how much consultation would be needed. The attorney's office said it would prepare and forward the retainer contract to the woman for signature. The woman received the contract but did not sign it because it was not what they had discussed in the consultation. The woman proceeded to meet with the attorney after sending her a draft of her agreement and obtained feedback and suggestions. The woman used 3 hours of the attorney's time and when the woman called to request that the excess funds be returned, the attorney said that was not what was in the agreement. The woman wrote a detailed account of their meeting, what was agreed to, the number of hours used and the disappointment she felt in the firm's lack of compassion and level of service provided during this extremely difficult life transition.*

The woman received a refund less the amount of hours rendered within a week. There was no apology given or acknowledgement of the miscommunication.

> **Please note: Every profession has individuals who are more competent and ethical than others. Take the time to find the right fit for you and your situation. Researching a Collaborative Law Association of professionals in your area is a good start.**

Notes/questions for your attorney:

_____

_____

_____

_____

_____

Disclosure Provision:

This provision is of utmost importance because it provides protection and recourse in the event that any assets were withheld or misrepresented for any reason.

Items to Consider:

- When mediating or engaging in the litigation process, you are relying on the honesty of the other party and reasonable knowledge that all assets and liabilities have been properly disclosed and shared. <u>This is where the use of a CDFA or forensic professional can be of great value and assistance in assuring that all financial information and marital assets have been properly disclosed.</u>

<u>Example 1 Sample Clause:</u>

Each party warrants to the other that he or she has made a full and complete disclosure as to his or her financial status. Each has informed the other as to all assets, real or personal, tangible or intangible, in which each party has any interest, legal or equitable. Further, each has made disclosure as to the reasonable worth or market value of such assets. These assets include interests in pension, profit sharing and/or retirement benefits; real estate; all business interests; all life insurance; all medical casualty, disability or other insurance coverage; all cash or other deposit accounts; all stocks, stock options, bonds and/or mutual funds; all tangible personal property, including household furnishings, appliances, art, jewelry, tools, equipment. A complete disclosure as to all income or other funds received by each from any source has been provided. In the event that a later determination of any material misrepresentation or omission with respect to the financial condition as described above, then such material misrepresentation or omission may be the basis for determination that this agreement is null and void.

If and in the event that either party fails to disclose the existence of any material property, the parties shall be entitled to make application to the court for an equitable distribution and sue the other party for damages under this Agreement in the amount equal to or greater than his or her marital interest in the undisclosed property and shall also be entitled to recover his or her reasonable attorney's fees.

Example 2 Sample Clause:

Each party hereto confirms that this Agreement identifies in some manner (even if by general referral) all of the marital assets or liabilities held by either of the parties individually or the parties' jointly. Each party confirms they have given the other party true and accurate information regarding assets of the marriage which are held in either party's sole name. In the event, however, that either Husband or Wife has failed to disclose to the other the existence of any marital property subject to equitable distribution or division under the laws of the State of XXXX or any other jurisdiction, the party whose rights have been prejudiced thereby, in addition to other remedies provided by law and equity, shall be entitled to make application to the court under the laws of the State of XXXX or any other jurisdiction or sue the other party for damages under this Agreement in an amount at least equal to his or her marital interest in the undisclosed property and shall also be entitled to recover his or her reasonable attorney's fees.

Example 3 Sample Clause:

The parties have agreed to the following:

A. Each party has made a full and fair disclosure to the other of his or her assets, liabilities, and income. Each party confirms that this Agreement identifies all of the marital assets and liabilities held by either of the parties individually or the parties jointly. Each party affirms that the other party has been given accurate written and verbal information regarding all assets and debts of the marriage which are held jointly or in either party's sole name.

B. Should either party fail to disclose any marital asset having a value exceeding $500.00 or any marital debt exceeding the sum of $500.00, the aggrieved party shall have the option to sue the non-disclosing party in contract under this agreement and if successful, shall be entitled to be awarded 100% of the value of any undisclosed asset and if a marital debt is at issue, 100% of the debt shall be charged to the non-disclosing party. In addition, the prevailing party shall be entitled to an award of reasonable attorney fees and court costs.

Evaluation: All of these clauses provide protection and remedies for any material misrepresentation of information.

Notes/questions for your attorney:

_____

_____

_____

_____

_____

Life Insurance: There are many reasons that it is prudent to consider life insurance on the primary income provider. It may be needed to cover alimony and/or child-related care costs as well as provide for income in the event that the primary income provider becomes disabled or dies. Please note that courts cannot order that life insurance needs to be provided. This is a negotiable item, which is clearly relevant to all concerned.

> *The amount of life insurance needed and length of time required is best determined by your financial planner or other professional as recommended by your attorney.*

Personal Priorities:

- What are you trying to accomplish with a life and/or disability insurance policy?

- Are you trying to cover child support and alimony until the children reach a certain age?
- Are you trying to provide security in the event of your death as well as provide an investment benefit for the future?

Items to Consider:

- Make sure your agreement is clear on who is the owner of the policy, who the beneficiaries are and who has the right to make changes to designated beneficiaries.

Example 1 Sample Clause:

So long as XXXX has an alimony obligation to XXXX, he shall keep in full force and effect his current term life insurance policy through Met Life which has a death benefit of $100,000. XXXX shall be designated as the beneficiary of this policy until XXXX alimony obligation is satisfied in full.

Example 2 Sample Clause:

Husband shall maintain a life insurance policy on both Husband's and Wife's life for the benefit of the minor children. Husband will be the sole and separate owner of all Life Insurance policies. Wife waives, renounces, and relinquishes any and all interest she may have in said policies.

> **Suggestion:** Whoever benefits from having the insurance policy should be the owner of the policy to ensure all premiums are being paid timely and that no changes can be made to the beneficiary designation.

Example 3 Sample Clause:

Husband shall be owner and shall carry a life insurance policy or death benefit of $1,000,000.00 on himself with the beneficiary designated as

Wife until June 15, 2018. In the event that Wife requests evidence of insurance that demonstrates Husband's compliance with this provision, Husband shall provide such evidence within 14 days of the request.

Wife shall be owner and shall carry a life insurance policy or death benefit of $1,000,000.00 on herself with the beneficiary designated as Husband until June 15, 2018. In the event that Husband requests evidence of insurance that demonstrates Wife's compliance with this provision, Wife shall provide such evidence within 14 days of the request.

Example 4 Sample Clause:

XXXX is the owner of a policy which has a cash surrender value of $82,687.04 as of June 12, 20xx. The policy has a death benefit of $xxxx. Upon execution of this Agreement, XXXX shall surrender this policy for the cash value which the parties will equally divide upon receipt of the surrender value proceeds, net of any capital gains taxes which will be equally shared.

Evaluation: Each of these clauses addresses different situations and objectives. Please discuss the necessity of a life insurance policy with a professional and/or your attorney.

Notes/questions for your attorney:

_____

_____

_____

_____

_____

Costs and Fees in the Event of Breach:

Example 1 Sample Clause:

If either party wrongfully violates the terms and conditions of this agreement and fails to perform his or her financial or other obligations to the other party, and as a result the other party incurs an expense, including reasonable attorney's fees and court costs incurred in the enforcement of this Agreement, the defaulting party shall indemnify and hold the other party harmless by paying for said expenses.

Example 2 Sample Clause:

In the event it becomes necessary to institute legal action to enforce compliance with the terms of this Agreement, to interpret this Agreement, or by reason of the breach by either party of this Agreement, then the parties agree that at the conclusion of such legal proceeding the breaching party shall be solely responsible for all legal fees and costs incurred by either party, such fees and costs to be taxed by the court. The amount so awarded shall be in the sole discretion of the presiding judge and the award shall be made without regard to the financial ability of either party to pay, but rather shall be based upon the fees and expenses determined by the court to be reasonable and incurred by the prevailing party. It is the intent of this paragraph to induce both Sam and Lisa to comply fully with the terms of this Agreement to the end that no litigation as between the parties is necessary in the areas dealt with by this Agreement. In the event of litigation, it is the further intent to specifically provide that the losing party pays all reasonable fees and costs that either side may incur.

Must Have!

Evaluation: Both sample clauses provide a clear understanding of the consequences if the parties do not abide by the agreements made in their contract. This is a "Must Have" clause!

Modification and/or Amendment of this Agreement:

This clause is to establish guidelines in the event that the parties' agreement needs to be modified or amended based on evolving circumstances or new information.

Example 1 Sample Clause:

If either party wishes to modify this Agreement, the other spouse will agree to mediate prior to litigation. The cost of the mediation will be shared equally by the parties. The terms of this Agreement may only be amended in writing, signed by both parties and notarized according to the law. No failure of a party to enforce or perform this Agreement exactly as written shall constitute a waiver or alteration of the term and shall not stop the party from enforcing the term in the future.

Evaluation: This clause requires the parties to mediate prior to litigation and that the cost will be shared by the parties. This requirement that mediation is required and the costs must be shared is not recommended as this wording may pose additional stress and controversy.

Example 2 Sample Clause:

This Agreement can be altered and amended only by further written duly executed by the parties. Any failure by either party to specifically perform or to enforce performance exactly according to the letter of this Agreement shall not constitute an alteration of the same by way of enlargement, waiver, reduction, estoppel, or otherwise, unless confirmed in writing by the parties. It is understood that the parties may, by mutual agreement, make temporary modifications from time to time as conditions require, but this Agreement shall nonetheless be binding upon the parties as written, except in the event of a material breach.

Evaluation: This clause is clear and concise as it is inevitable that minor circumstances will change and have to be addressed accordingly.

Example 3 Sample Clause:

This Agreement can be altered and amended only by further formal written agreement duly executed by the parties. Any failure by either party to specifically perform or enforce performance exactly according to the letter of this Agreement shall not constitute an alteration of the same by way of enlargement, reduction, estoppel or otherwise, unless confirmed in writing by the parties and duly executed by both parties. It is understood that the parties may, by mutual agreement, make temporary modifications from time to time as conditions require but that, absent a further formal written agreement duly executed by the parties, this Agreement shall be binding upon the parties as written. No custom or practice which may develop between the parties in the course of the performance of this Agreement shall be construed as a waiver of the right of either party to insist upon compliance with the provisions hereof by the other.

Items to Consider:

- As circumstances change, many clauses will need adjustment based on the situation at hand. Please discuss alternatives with your attorney and ensure that you have a clear understanding of how these items can be addressed.

Notes/questions for your attorney:

_____

_____

_____

_____

Payment of Professional Fees:

The attorney and other professional fees associated with drafting this agreement and procuring the final non-contested divorce, including court costs, shall be paid by the parties equally (or as otherwise agreed to). Individual financial, legal or other advice for each party's benefit shall be the responsibility of the person seeking it.

Evaluation: There are instances where professional fees may be able to be recouped from an opposing party. Discuss your situation with your attorney.

Notes/questions for your attorney:

_____

_____

_____

_____

_____

Tax Returns:

Example 1 Sample Clause:

In the event that Steve and Donna are audited by the IRS or State Agency for a tax year in which they filed jointly, any costs relating to personal taxes associated with such an audit including, but not limited to, back taxes, interest, penalties, and legal/accounting fees will be shared equally (or as designated).

Evaluation: If either party intentionally concealed income from the IRS, the opposite party may have an "innocent spouse" defense from any additional liability.

Example 2 Sample Clause:

For the 201X tax year, the parties shall file separate income tax returns. It is agreed and understood that neither party has the right to sign the other's name on any forms, and particularly on any tax-related forms or checks. In the event of any assessment of a deficiency in any income tax filing for any year for which a joint return is or has been filed, Husband and Wife shall equally pay the deficiency. In the event any refund is due for tax year 201X or any prior year that a joint return was filed, the parties shall equally divide the refund.

Items to Consider:

- Consult with your attorney, as there are many items to consider based on your individual situation, such as if you were aware of all claims and assertions used in preparing these returns; if you have been audited in the past; and/or if you own your own business.

Notes/questions for your attorney:

_____

_____

_____

_____

_____

Fairness of Settlement/Future Claims:

Example 1 Sample Clause:

The parties expressly acknowledge and agree that the division and distribution of marital property, divisible property, and marital debts set forth herein, although not exactly equal, is just, fair, equitable, and reasonable. The parties intend for their Agreement to bind each of them. Each party expressly waives any and all other rights, whether now in existence or hereafter acquired, to claim equitable distribution under laws of (State: XXX) or any other jurisdiction. This Agreement may be pleaded in bar of any such claim for relief in any suit or arbitration hereafter filed.

Example 2 Sample Clause:

As provided herein, the parties have already divided between themselves and to their mutual satisfaction, all assets owned and liabilities owed by them individually and jointly. Each party hereby waives, releases and relinquishes unto the other any and all right, title and interest in the property herein above assigned to the other. Hereafter, neither party shall make any claim against the other inconsistent wit this Agreement for any property assigned to the other hereunder or for any property currently held in the name of the other party.

Warranty Regarding Reading Before Execution:

Example 1 Sample Clause:

Both parties warrant and agree that they have read and understand this Agreement and its contents; that they have sought such professional counsel as they deem appropriate before signing; that it is a fair and reasonable agreement for each of them, having regard to the condition and circumstances of the parties on the date hereof; that each has signed this Agreement voluntarily without duress, fear, compulsion, persuasion, or undue influence by the other party or any other persons.

Example 3 Sample Clause:

Each party acknowledges that he/she has read this Agreement and understands its content and provisions; that it is a fair and reasonable agreement to each of them, having due regard to the conditions and circumstances of the parties hereto on the date hereof; that each has signed and executed the Agreement freely and voluntarily and without fear, compulsion, duress, coercion, persuasion or undue influence exercised by either party upon the other or by any other person or persons upon either.

Items to Consider:

- Here is another disclaimer of responsibility by the assisting professional and a reminder that you are a legal adult and have the right to choose whether to have professional counsel.
- This further emphasizes the importance of understanding your agreement in entirety and engaging professionals that can assist in this process.

Indemnity Agreement:
Example 1 Sample Clause:

In the future, if an action is instituted against Husband arising out of any indebtedness in which Husband or any corporation, partnership, or limited liability company is the principal obligor or with respect to which Husband has otherwise guaranteed the same, Husband agrees to indemnify and hold Wife harmless from and against any and all liability with respect to any such indemnified obligations.

In the future, if an action is instituted against Wife arising out of any indebtedness in which Wife or any corporation, partnership, or limited liability company is the principal obligor or with respect to which Wife has otherwise guaranteed the same, Wife agrees to indemnify and hold Husband harmless from and against any and all liability with respect to any such indemnified obligations.

Example 2 Sample Clause:

Each party warrants to the other that he or she shall not seek from the other contribution for the payment of expenses for necessaries that he or she may incur. As long as the parties are married, each party warrants that at any time services for necessaries are rendered, he or she shall provide actual notice to any third party who provides necessaries to him or her that he or she is legally separated from the other party and that said provider should have no expectation of compensation or reimbursement from the other party by virtue of the parties' marriage. Each party agrees to indemnify, defend, and hold the other harmless from and against third-party creditors who seek compensation from him or her under the doctrine of necessaries under the present and future laws of any jurisdiction.

Must Have!

Items to Consider:

This clause refers to the period of time that the couple is separated but not yet divorced. The most common type of debt that may be incurred during this time period is for credit cards or medical expenses. <u>It is most prudent to ensure that all assets and liabilities are transferred to the designated individual and that all debt is refinanced and or transferred to the responsible party prior to or in conjunction with the signing of your agreement.</u>

Notes/questions for your attorney:

_____

_____

_____

_____

_____

Specific Performance:

Either party shall have the right to compel the performance of the provisions of this Agreement by suing for specific performance in the courts where jurisdiction of the parties and subject matter exists. Both parties acknowledge that neither party has a plain, speedy or adequate legal remedy to compel compliance with the provisions of this Agreement, that neither party shall be required to repeatedly file suit for any breach of this Agreement, that this Agreement is fair and equitable to both parties, and that an order of specific performance enforceable by contempt is an appropriate remedy for a breach of this Agreement by either party. The right to specific performance of this Agreement shall be in addition to and not in substitution for all other rights and remedies either party may have at law or in equity arising by reason of any breach of the Agreement by the non-complying party. In the event either party files an action for Specific Performance, the parties may opt to use Arbitration to resolve the outstanding issues. In the event the parties mutually agree to arbitration at the time, each party shall choose one arbitrator and the arbitrators shall mutually agree on a third arbitrator.

The three arbitrators chosen shall then hear such issues as exist at that time and the results of such arbitration shall be binding.

Items to Consider:

- What is the cost benefit of clarifying an item?
- This is why it is imperative that the language in your agreement be as specific as possible to avoid any future chaos and discord.

True Story: A couple had entered into an agreement with a specific clause that identified addition expenses for child-related expenses that would be paid by each party. Even though the couple outlined these expenses, the cost to require specific performance far outweighed the amount of reimbursement required.

PART III

Moving on with dignity and grace

CHAPTER 7
Moving Forward

This chapter has been broken down into two separate perspectives from the author and the consulting attorney based on their personal experiences and passion for those dealing with this difficult and formidable life transition.

A: Insights, viewpoints and encouragement from Author Jacqueline Eddy

*"You either **get bitter** or you **get better**. It's that simple. You either take what has been dealt to you and allow it to make you a better person, or you allow it to tear you down. **The choice does not belong to fate, it belongs to you.**"*

-Josh Shipp

Easier said than done, right? Your life has been turned upside down or maybe it was your choice to separate; nevertheless, there will be challenges to overcome. There will be adjustments needed emotionally and financially to be able to move forward in a graceful and more manageable manner. Many of the emotional challenges we face include:

- Am I a failure?

- Will I have a good second marriage?
- Have I learned and grown from this relationship?
- Where do I begin?
- Do I like myself?
- Am I proud of my behavior, actions and the way I treat others?
- Does my perception of myself match that of my reputation?
- Do I have faith or courage to make my life and the life of those around me a better place?

Of course, this significant life transition will come with fears, doubts, guilt, relief and negativity. And, if you truly want to move forward and not recreate the same mistakes, take time to review the following exercises and information to help you move into a positive direction.

Goals and Gratitude

One of the best tools to bring about positive change is practicing *Gratitude!* With each and every passing day, when you make a deliberative effort to be grateful, you will feel lighter, more peaceful and secure about your future.

Try not to focus on what got you here, whose fault it was or the unfairness of the situation, but on the future possibilities. Some days you will shake your fist at the heavens, cry yourself to sleep or alienate everyone around you. There are many people who have been in your situation or worse, and while that is no consolation, it is a seed of hope. You can overcome this situation and be happy.

Negativity only attracts more negativity.

In the book, *Well Being – The Five Essential Elements*, the author refers to the achievement of wellbeing and that it is accomplished by giving energy to these five essential elements: Career Wellbeing (how you occupy your time or simply liking what you do every day), Social Wellbeing (having strong relationships and love/friendship in your life), Financial Wellbeing (effectively managing your economic life), Physical Wellbeing (having good health and enough energy to get things done on a daily basis) and Community Wellbeing (sense of engagement you have with the area where you live).

On pages 6-7, the book states that statistics show that "While 66% of people are doing well in at least one of these areas, just 7% are thriving in all five. If we're struggling in any one of these domains, as most of us are, it damages our wellbeing and wears on our daily life. When we strengthen our wellbeing in any of these areas, we will have better days, months, and decades. But we're not getting the most out of our lives unless we're living effectively in all five."

Many people get so caught up in things they have no control over. So, decide for yourself that you will choose each and every day to be grateful and that you will *DO* something!

With that in mind, I've outlined a little exercise below that you might find interesting and that will help you to engage more effectively in all areas of your wellbeing! The rewards can be invaluable.

Exercise:
Buy yourself a little notebook and do the following:

Daily

Each morning, record the date, 5 things that make you grateful and 3 daily goals: one for home/work; one that can be completed that day related to family/loved one; and one specifically related to you.

Weekly

Complete 2 additional goals related to managing your finances and your relationship with your community or neighbors.

At the end of each day/week, review your goals, see if you have completed them and write yes or no next to them. Be positive and supportive of yourself. Close your eyes, visualize good times and reject all negativity that may try to consume you. Repeat the same steps the following day/ week and be creative for the things you are grateful/thankful for! Have fun with this!

While at first this task may seem simplistic, *you will be amazed at the personal satisfaction you will feel at the end of the day when you can say "Yes, I completed ALL my goals today."*

Don't be discouraged if at first you are not accomplishing what you set out to do. Tomorrow is another day and it will be another wonderful opportunity! A pattern will begin to develop. You will begin to notice the goals you consistently complete and those where you need to make more effort to be balanced.

Example:
Date: June 24, 2015

Grateful for: (Be Creative with new things)
This beautiful day!
Cheerios
My friends
The flowers in the garden
The smell of coffee

Goals for the day:
I will book flights to see my parents.
I will make 6 sales calls.
I will walk the neighborhood loop two times.

Weekly Goals:

- Review Sunday bulletin and sign up for an activity or make a contribution to a cause. Please note: While both goals are important, you will receive more personal satisfaction from a hands-on activity.
- Review your budget and make necessary adjustments or set a new savings goal.

Other examples include: Making and delivering sandwiches to the poor, shopping with a friend for a clothes drive, assisting with a community clean up, volunteering at a local school, reviewing your budget, making adjustments to your budget, start saving for a new goal, meeting with an advisor, reviewing your insurance needs and premiums, and getting quotes.

> **During the beginning stages of the divorce process, many people become anxious and agitated because nothing seems to be getting accomplished. Many feel they are in "limbo" and then when the divorce is final, they struggle with finding a new direction. Having little goals and focusing on the things you can control will ease this burden.**

Personal Direction and Clarity

As it was mentioned in the introduction, a great deal of loss is experienced when a marriage fails. In many cases, it is not about the loss of a particular person but the loss of a dream or unmet expectations. There will be a natural progression from fear and sadness to anger to relief to peace and happiness. While you might find this difficult to do at this time, it is in your best interest to try to think of your future as well as for those of any children you have. Believe that you deserve to be happy and be loved!

Ask yourself the following questions:

Personal Preferences or Purpose:

- Describe what you do best and why. Relax and write whatever comes to mind. It may be gardening, reading to your children, organizing a project, developing staff, giving presentations, social media, and/or cooking. Relax and admire yourself!
- Are you currently doing some of these tasks regularly?
- Are there things you would like to try or wish you were doing more often?

Values and Priorities:

- What is most important to you in life and in your work?
- For each of the 8 areas listed below, write what you care about most in each area. Try to write something even if you are unsure.
  - Career:
  - Health:
  - Money:
  - Spirituality:
  - Personal Development:
  - Recreation:
  - Physical Environment (work & personal):

Self-Awareness:

List 5 attributes about yourself that you would consider a strength or that you love/like about yourself. Be your own cheerleader! Then, list 3-5 attributes that you would consider a weakness. (Any areas identified as a weakness do not necessarily mean you have to "fix" anything, but it will provide awareness of when you need to reach out to others who can assist you.)

Needs:

Right now I feel the greatest sense of need for.......
The problems or challenges I most want to overcome right now are.....
The place I feel stuck is.......

Share this information with your counselor or a friend. Focus on the things that make you happy. With the information above, create a *"Visual Story Board"* with each of these areas and place pictures from your own inventory or from magazines. This exercise will give you happiness and inspiration every time you look at it! It is a fun process to do with a friend. Sharing and voicing your goals and desires brings them that much closer to you!

Many clients or friends were stuck at first and did not know how to begin or felt silly or vulnerable. This simple task has been a source of inspiration to myself and many of my clients and friends. I am on my third visual storyboard. As I achieve certain dreams or priorities change, I revisit my board and recreate it. I have done this about once a year. This idea was taken from a mutual friend and the Author of *Next Level Living: Today's Guide for Tomorrow's Abundant Life,* Linda McLean.

Be mindful of your thoughts and the company you keep.

"Freedom is what you do with what's been done to you." – Jean Paul Sartre

While it will be natural to have feelings of resentment or anger, do not let these emotions interfere with your future happiness. You can get stuck in the blame game, feeling sorry for yourself or competing with your former partner for the kids' attention or approval. This is where you need to take a step back and look at the environment you created for yourself. All you can do is your best to be positive and happy. *Positivity is contagious! And so is negativity! What will you choose?*

- Do you associate with people who build you up or bring you down?
- Are there people who, just by being around them, make the room and all those they meet a better place?
- Do you have faith that gives you comfort and peace?
- Are you happy being alone or do you need constant attention?
- Do you continually rehash the wrongs that have been done to you?

Creating healthy boundaries is important for a happy life. Write a list of 4-5 people you enjoy being around and why. Are they positive, kind, generous and happy? What qualities do you admire and why? Take inventory of the people that you share your time with. Start to make changes. Reduce the amount of time spent with people who bring you down or only provide entertainment.

> *If personal confrontation with your former spouse*
> *is uncomfortable, limit that interaction to email or*
> *texting to the best of your ability given your situation.*

Stay positive and seek to surround yourself with those who build you up or who you have positive interaction with. Hopefully, this will give you insight to the people who make you feel bad about yourself or uncomfortable. Each of us needs to find our own way and the process is easier when you have good people and influences around you. Let me give you a couple examples from my own life of those who inspired me:

My mother, who was very reserved, devout catholic, loved her family and enjoyed sharing their joys. She was a wonderful and caring wife and loved reading and sharing little stories from Reader's Digest. She was kind and patient and did not require a lot of things! She was always a pleasure to be around. While she had no material accomplishments to set her apart, she was always there for her own children and many others who needed to be uplifted in some way! She was an expert at keeping life simple but fulfilling!

My former spouse's Aunt Peggy is the epitome of positivity! She creates an environment where everyone always feels welcome and giddy! She is an accomplished artist, activity planner and generous friend to all. She always seems to handle adversity with ease! You can feel her energy for days even after she is gone.

My best friend, Sharon, is indeed someone who tirelessly listened for years and still listens to me as I rebuild my life personally and financially. She is one who selflessly and consistently encouraged me in my work endeavors; my relationships with my children, stepchildren, and husband; and the emotional adjustments experienced when creating a new family dynamic.

In the midst of all this change, we can overwhelm ourselves. Sometimes we need to take a big breath! And this can mean taking a break from our selves. I began volunteering at my church, and while at first I chose to do this to keep busy while my children were not in my care, I quickly found that I enjoyed helping others and the people I worked with were genuine, relaxing, purposeful and positive. I felt a sense of accomplishment. It took my mind off of me!!!!! And it was a great vacation!

Who inspires you? Who do you admire?

Taking the time to review and evaluate with whom you spend your time and how you direct your energy will have a significant impact on the quality and happiness of your life.

Post Divorce Financial Challenges

For most couples, there is a significant change to financial means to which each is accustomed. This is further complicated when there are children involved. Financial stress brings about resentment and fear. These attributes bring about more stress and chaos. Financial challenges you may face include:

- Creating a budget
- Paying bills and making financial decisions

- Making financial goals or plans
- Planning for unanticipated events

If you engaged the services of a CDFA, many of these items were discussed in detail during the course of the divorce process. Listed below is a brief overview of these items and a few reminders or recommendations to avoid future discord.

Creating a Budget

When you are divorcing, it is imperative to create and learn to follow a budget—the more detailed the better. Based upon the amount of available cash to provide or receive child support or alimony, each party will have to adjust to these new circumstances. Having a detailed and accurate budget will help get you started. If you find yourself not adhering to your budgeted amounts, *it is easier to correct now than trying to catch up later*. Be prudent in reviewing your expenses until you become accustomed to your new standard of living.

While many couples with children initially try to overcompensate for the change in living arrangements with monetary distractions or trying to be the "fun" parent, this ultimately does more harm than good to all parties. The increased financial stress will eventually affect everyone, as well as the disappointment when the increased attention/expenditures is/are no longer provided consistently.

Paying Bills and Making Financial Decisions

Hopefully, you have already established a separate account to pay your bills independently. Based on the due dates of your monthly bills and when you will receive payments or make payments, you may have to call your credit card companies or utilities to adjust the due dates to meet your obligations when they become due easier. While you may receive a set monthly amount, certain expenses are to be paid quarterly or annually and these amounts should be transferred to savings or set aside to be available when payment is due.

Car insurance and homeowner insurance rates should be reviewed and compared every year to ensure you are receiving the best pricing. If circumstances change, you should be able to adjust your budget accordingly. If you have been prudently monitoring your expenses, you will be able to make adjustments with ease.

Making Financial Goals or Plans

Making financial goals will give you security and confidence in yourself. It is highly recommended that you interview and meet with a minimum of 3 financial planners to help to understand your financial goals, fees and options available to you. Based on your agreement, you may/will have investment options.

Unanticipated Events

Some items that are consistently overlooked are payments that are required quarterly or annually, such as:

- Personal taxes on vehicles – paid on an annual basis
- Insurance payments – can be paid monthly, quarterly or annually
- Payment of school activities, supplies and clothes – Usually these items are seasonal and must be budgeted and saved for
- Repairs and maintenance

If these items were included in your budget, then these amounts should already be saved for when payment becomes due.

Last but not least – FAITH.........

*"I want you **to experience the riches of your salvation:** Joy of being loved constantly and perfectly. You make a practice of judging yourself, based on how you look or behave or feel. If you like what you see in the mirror, you feel a bit more **worthy of My Love**. When things are going smoothly and your performance seems adequate, you find it easier to believe **you are My beloved***

child. When you feel discouraged, you tend to look inward so you can correct whatever is wrong.

*Instead of trying to "fix" yourself, fix your gaze on Me, **the Lover of your soul**. Rather than using your energy to judge yourself, redirect it to praising Me. Remember that I see you **clothed in My righteousness**, radiant in My perfect Love."*

-Jesus Calling, Sarah Young, page 204

Faith is a funny thing. It is so personal, and it is the root of all goodness in our lives, our communities, and even our government. The foundation of our existence relies solely in the goodwill shown to our selves, our families and our communities.

While faith can provide peace and direction, we must be open to this phenomenon and give ourselves completely to the One who knows what is best for us. This doesn't mean that we can't pray and ask for things. It only means that if we don't get the things we ask for that we need to trust in God's plans for us.

"Trust" in God. This is an unexplainable and sometimes extremely controversial concept.

By definition: Trust (noun)

1. Reliance on the integrity, strength, ability, surety, etc., of a person or thing; confidence.
2. Confident expectation of something; hope.

If hope is lost, what is left? If you have never prayed or gone to church, give it a try.

There are many churches, divorce groups and counseling centers that can assist you as you process this change. Do not be afraid to ask for help! Find what works best for you. Incorporating faith into your life will help you find balance, peace and happiness. There will come a point in time when you will begin to face your fears and know that you will be all right. You will start to believe in yourself. You will know that you deserve respect, and the unknown will no longer be as scary as it was before. This realization happens at different times for everyone, but it will happen!

In Summary:

There will be some individuals who feel divorce is not a big deal and that everyone does it, or at least 50% of the population anyway. While our culture is becoming more accepting of this trend, it does not mean it is what the majority wants. If you asked couples getting married if divorce were an option, most would be aghast! Later, many become disenchanted and seek the dream elsewhere. This is probably why the divorce rate is significantly higher for second and third marriages. Those individuals will probably not even read this chapter.

The point is anyone can benefit from gratitude, self-evaluation, goal setting and being mindful of your thoughts and the company you keep. Sharing your life with someone who loves you, encourages you and accepts you is a blessing, and it is a huge reward when you can be that to another person as well. Each and every person is different and will require varying amounts of time to rebuild themselves. We encourage you to take the time to feel good about yourself, evaluate your environment and the way you treat others, so that you will have a beautiful and bright future with or without a new partner!

While I have shared a brief overview of the emotional and financial challenges many face during and after the divorce and some exercises and resources to help you move forward, I want to personally wish you success and strength for a happy future.

B: Insights, viewpoints and encouragement
from Consulting Attorney, Marshall Karro

The most frequent impediment to resolving issues arising from a separation is the inability of one or both parties to think objectively and rationally. This is understandable, since there are few things in life that fuel emotional thinking more than personal conflict. Most separations are characterized by feelings of distrust and resentment. Blame is typically not in short supply. In many instances the urge to try and inflict pain on the other side by implementing a combative and accusatorial approach (i.e., litigation) in a public forum (i.e., courtroom) where each party's attorney will have the opportunity to provide a "day of reckoning" takes priority over a more "solutions-oriented" approach where certain accommodations are necessary to resolve issues.

Since experienced trial attorneys are well trained in litigation techniques and are confident in their ability to "win issues," their focus is often on prevailing as an advocate rather than on the damage that might be inflicted on family relationships by putting husband and wives, who are often mothers and fathers, through an adversarial process where each sides' poor choices as either a spouse, parent or both are brought to light in a courtroom. The outcome may in some considerable measure be the result of subjective thinking by the judge as to whose case seems more compelling. In any event, both sides lose control of the result and put it in the hands of a judge who may have little experience in family court or whose thinking may be slanted one way or the other based upon that judge's particular life experience and resulting mindset. Obviously, different personalities see things differently. Do you really want to have your rights to property, support and custody of children determined by someone whose thinking may be entirely different from your own?

A collaborative approach is solutions oriented and is designed to allow both sides to discuss issues in a civil and respectful manner and to listen to and hopefully give some recognition to a point of view other than your own in coming to a resolution with which both sides have enough of a comfort level so that neither feels he or she has lost and the other has won.

In my experience, there is significant value in bringing personal conflict to closure since it is clearly a source of tension and anxiety, which effects not only the parties but also spills over to affect the lives of children. Family dysfunction is exacerbated by ongoing conflict, and the message to children is that mom and dad are unable to solve problems (which exist between them), so how can they be a good resource to solve problems which arise as a child matures into adulthood?

If I can render any intelligent advice to people undergoing the turmoil of separation it would be to retain control of the decisions to be made, rather than surrendering such control to a judge and to recognize that there is significant value to removing personal conflict from your life through means other than a protracted adversarial process.

CHAPTER 8
Conclusion

Throughout this book, we have tried to emphasize the importance of proper guidance from <u>third-party professionals</u> based on your individual situation, give you an overview of the divorce process and things you will need to address, sample clauses to review and some real situations we have encountered with our clients. We cannot emphasize enough the importance of this life transition and that there are champions for a fair and equitable settlement for the entire family. The best advice as we can offer is to engage and/or consult with a Collaborative Law Attorney and allow a CDFA to review your financial situation. No matter how simplistic you may feel your situation is, all agreements should be reviewed with an attorney to ensure there are no gray areas or interpretations that could cause further chaos or discord.

In Wellbeing: The Five Essential Elements, the authors point out that if we involve others in our efforts to improve, we double or triple our chances of success. This applies to the negotiation process of divorce itself (others include attorneys, mediators, coaches, CDFAs, and financial advisors).

> *As stated in the introduction, the reality of the legal parameters and the numbers help address and manage expectations!*

I hope you were surprised by the analysis provided in Appendix A. Each situation is different and not until you *"Run"* the numbers can you see the benefits or options available to each party. By being open minded and creative, there can be inherent benefits to each party. Whether you like it or not, you will be required to have interaction and communication with your former spouse when children are involved for many years. <u>This is basically your one and only chance to get an agreement that is clear, detailed and financially sound for the entire family.</u> While you may have the option to mediate if there is confusion, this will only cost more money and create further stress. Or worse, the cost-benefit of arguing a specific clause will not outweigh clarification of the issue and you will have to live with the results because it was not clear enough to begin with.

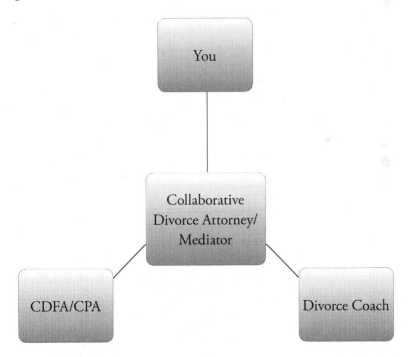

If you are still uncertain of how you should proceed, ask yourself this question: When I look back at this time in my life, will I be proud how I handled myself, gathered information and sought quality experts and professionals to assist me through the divorce process? It is your life; make the most of it!

We sincerely hope that this book has been of value to you and your situation. We wish you happiness and strength for a new and beautiful life!

APPENDIX A
Sample Case Scenario

Actual Case Scenario:

The clients used for purposes of this example had a very adversarial relationship and chose to only communicate through their attorneys. The husband had an attorney who also had a collaborative law attorney designation and the wife went through several attorneys and incurred significant legal fees for a number of reasons. Unfortunately, the process took longer than expected, primarily because the parties were unwilling to accept that they were not going to be able to live in the same manner they were used to in separate households. Combined they spent nearly $53,000 in legal fees and other professional services.

Background: The couple has 2 children, currently in private school. The wife had been a stay at-home mom for several years and has just recently reinstated her nursing certificate and secured a nursing position. While the couple was at odds about their financial situation, they **both** felt very strongly about providing for their children's education and activities. While these are good intentions, the couple had to make serious adjustments because their financial situation would not allow either party or their children to live separately in the manner to which they were accustomed. To save money, the couple has been living together throughout the negotiation process.

To begin the process, each party prepared a budget of his/her monthly expenses and the husband also provided a detailed listing of marital assets. The couple did not want to liquidate any of its marital assets to cover living expenses and could not understand why there was not enough income to allocate. This is where the collaborative law attorney suggested that the couple work with a CDFA to help the clients understand their financial situation and options. Most clients need a financial picture to manage their expectations before they spend a lot of time, money and incur a great deal of stress.

To keep costs down and demonstrate the benefits of having a financial evaluation, we simply prepared a Net Income After Expenses and Taxes based on their separate budgets, child support calculation and an estimated alimony amount of $1,000 to begin the process.

Taking this information and the estimated college expenses, car expenses and medical expenses that husband was considering assuming would have him in a negative cash flow for the next 10+ years thereby depleting any net worth that had accumulated. Likewise, the wife would be in the same position because there was not enough income to cover her expenses.

This was the projected income based on the budgets they prepared:

Projected Income	Husband	Wife
2018	($38,223)	($8,541)
2019	($64,541)	($10,208)
2020	($63,945)	($12,225)
2021	($45,188)	($21,938)
2022	($46,225)	($22,783)
2023	($51,621)	($24,641)
2024	($48,609)	($32,272)
2025	($43,354)	($47,481)
2026	($47,140)	($48,658)

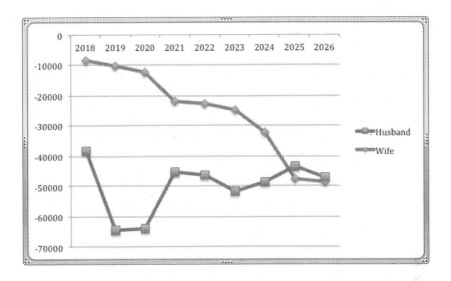

Based on this information, it is clear that each party will have to reduce his/her monthly living expenses, evaluate his/her living arrangements and reduce extraordinary children's expenses in order to plan for the future.

THIS FINANCIAL PICTURE ALLOWED EACH PARTY TO BE MORE OPEN AND COMPROMISING. THEY BOTH FINALLY REALIZED THE INHERENT BENEFIT OF REVIEWING THEIR FINANCIAL POSITION AND SCENARIOS THAT WOULD BE MORE MANAGEABLE FOR ALL PARTIES.

- The husband realized while he makes a good income, he cannot provide for everyone's needs and expect to retire.
- The wife realized that there is only so much income and will need to reconsider her budget and plan for when the income from child support and alimony will no longer be available.

The couple ultimately agreed to the following:
- Eliminate private schooling, reduce individual budgets and reduce and manage extracurricular activities for the children and amount of college expenses supplemented.

- The husband would move out of the marital home after divorce agreement was completed and rent until he could find something to purchase.
- The wife would stay in the marital home until the last child graduates because they had a low mortgage, they were in a good school district and it would not have been financially practical for the wife to rent or purchase a new home at this time.
- After the sale of the marital residence, wife purchases a new home. Both parties share in the equity of the marital home upon sale, but the husband gives more of the gain (40/60) split to wife so that wife can purchase a new home. Allocation of marital assets is still 50/50. Her income will still be supplemented by alimony for a few more years but projections show that wife will need a higher salary after alimony and child support ends.

Based on these adjustments, the resulting projected income after expenses for the couple is as follows:

Projected Income	Husband	Wife
2018	($43,482)	($ 793)
2019	($19,985)	$17,292
2020	($24,544)	$16,244
2021	($11,864)	$14,792
2022	($ 8,094)	$7,716
2023	($10,168)	$14,409
2024	$ 804	$13,323
2025	$11,308	$ 3,074
2026	$31,596	($19,648)
2027	$54,096	($22,705)
2028	$56,917	($23,574)

The husband feels more comfortable with this analysis because he is able to help his children, adjust for any decreases in salary as he ages and plan for the future. While some liquidations of investments may be required in the early years, the long-term benefits of preserving assets and having a plan is justified.

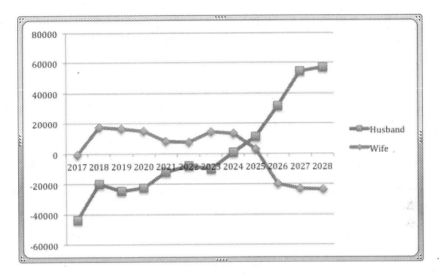

Based on a 50/50 split of their marital assets and the income projections above their projected net worth for future years is as follows:

Net Worth	Husband	Wife
2017	$553,487	$596,974
2018	$541,445	$639,778
2019	$524,352	$683,262
2020	$507,079	$727,097
2021	$507,675	$765,967
2022	$514,767	$806,134
2023	$509,433	$836,111
2024	$530,697	$886,488
2025	$563,480	$928,743
2026	$618,029	$949,096
2027	$697,432	$967,020
2028	$783,006	$984,716

2029	$875,135	$1,000,876
2030	$974,236	$1,016,614
2031	$1,080,783	$1,031,827

Both couples have the opportunity to work with a financial planner to maximize their investment strategy and contributions based on the years when they will have excess cash. A 4% interest rate of return was used in the information presented. If the wife does not increase her income she will begin using her invested assets.

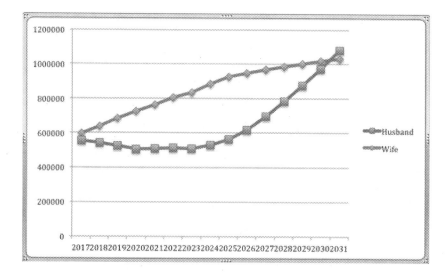

After presentation of this information, the couple was able to understand their situation better, the monies available, and the future impact and opportunities of this process.

Summary of Financial Analysis:

- The interest-based allocation of resources in this situation still allocates the net assets equally but allows for both parties to share in the expenses to sell the home and allows the wife to purchase another home and be approved for a loan, manage the children's extraordinary expenses and plan for the future. The couple realized based on this presentation that their budgets do not accommodate the payment of private school tuition and college expenses. The husband has agreed to assist the children as included in his budget and help them to obtain student loans as needed. **This will eliminate years of conflict and stress.**

- The divorce family law software that is used provides a wealth of information that incorporates the tax effects of transactions and the related impact on income, schedules detailing liquidations required to cover negative cash flow, interest rates and assumptions used in projections, detailed budgets, asset allocations and what-if scenarios.

Other Benefits include:

- The wife will be able to qualify based on her income to purchase another home and have funds for a down payment. This avoids the additional costs of renting or moving twice.
- The wife has the option of reevaluating her expenses and providing for her future. From the analysis, it is apparent that the wife will have to make adjustments to her living expenses after child support ends and then again when alimony is terminated. When purchasing a home, she will be able to review her situation and plan accordingly. The wife may need the assistance of another financial review or would benefit from the services of a CDFA who is also a financial planner. She will need to begin liquidation of assets to cover negative cash flow in the later years if income is not replaced.
- Payments on home will be made by the wife and any material costs or repairs will be reimbursed out of the proceeds of the home to the party who made any material repairs. All utilities will be transferred to wife's name. This will also allow her to establish credit on her own.

The information presented reveals that the husband will incur higher expenses in the early years and the wife will incur higher expenses in the later years when alimony is no longer being paid. Many couples who have $1,000,000 to $3,000,000 in assets have the most difficulty in separating their assets and establishing alimony because their income and assets preclude them from living in the same manner to which they were accustomed. **I hope this presentation of information proves the importance of The Collaborative Law Divorce Process and its inherent benefits to the entire family.**

THIS PRESENTATION OF INFORMATION HAS HELPED BOTH PARTIES MANAGE THEIR EXPECTATIONS AND PLAN FOR THEIR FUTURE. THEY BOTH AGREED THEY FELT MORE COMFORTABLE WITH THE ALLOCATION OF ASSETS AND THE DETAILS OF WHERE THE MONEY IS BEING SPENT.

For informational purposes, details of the allocation of their marital property is as follows:

	Husband	Wife	Total
Real Estate Equity			
Marital Home (net of mortgage)	$105,189	$157,783	$262,972
Lot Held for Investment	$138,000	$138,000	$276,000
(net of expenses; taxable gain included in their individual income projections)			
Total Real Estate Equity	$243,189	$295,783	$538,972
Cash & Investments			
CD	$ 5,000	$ 5,000	$ 10,000
Checking Acct.	$ 1,250	$ 1,250	$ 2,500
Savings Acct.	$ 4,000	$ 4,000	
Vanguard Retirement Acct.	$ 52,494	$ 52,494	$104,987
Total Investments	$ 58,744	$ 62,743	$121,487

Cars and Personal Effects

Wife Car	$ 18,000	$ 18,000	
Other personal property to be distributed as agreed by the parties			
Total Personal Items	$ 18,000	$ 18,000	
Subtotal Non-Retirement	**$301,933**	**$376,526**	**$678,459**
IRA/401ks			
United Health Group 401k	$172,688	$0	$172,688
Aetna 401k plan	$ 48,326	$221,014	$269,340
Total IRA/401ks	$221,014	$221,014	$442,028
Defined Benefit Pensions			
Defined Benefit Plan	$ 74,356	$0	$ 74,356
Total Pensions	$ 74,356	$0	$ 74,356
Subtotal Retirement	**$295,370**	**$221,014**	**$516,384**
Total Assets	**$597,303**	**$597,540**	**$1,194,843**
Debts			
Credit Card Debt	($13,229)	($13,229)	($26,457)
Total Debts	($13,229)	($13,229)	($26,457)
Total Assets	**$597,303**	**$597,540**	**$1,194,843**
Total Debts	**($13,229)**	**($13,229)**	**($26,457)**
Total Marital Property	**$584,074**	**$584,311**	**$1,168,386**

Note: "Total amount" column may not add due to rounding.

APPENDIX B
Collaborative Divorce Engagement Agreement

Principles and Guidelines for the Practice of Collaborative Law

I. <u>GOALS</u>

We acknowledge that the essence of "Collaborative Law" is the shared belief by participants that it is in the best interests of parties and their families in typical Family Law matters to commit themselves to avoiding litigation.

We therefore adopt this conflict resolution process, which does-not rely on a Court-imposed resolution, but relies on an atmosphere of honesty, cooperation, integrity and professionalism geared toward the future well-being of the family.

Our goal is to minimize, if not eliminate, the negative economic, social and emotional consequences of protracted litigation to the participants and their families.

We commit ourselves to the Collaborative Law process and agree to seek a better way to resolve our differences justly and equitably.

II. NO COURT OR OTHER INTERVENTION

We commit ourselves to settling our case without court intervention.

We agree to give full, honest and open disclosure of all information, whether requested or not.

We agree to engage in informal discussions and conferences to settle all issues.

We agree to direct all attorneys, accountants, therapists, appraisers and other consultants retained by us to work in a cooperative effort to resolve issues without resort to litigation or any other external decision making process except as agreed upon.

III. CAUTIONS

We understand there is no guarantee that the process will be successful in resolving our case.

We understand that the process cannot eliminate concerns about the disharmony, distrust and irreconcilable differences which have led to the current conflict.

We understand that we are still expected to assert our respective interests and that our respective attorneys will help each of us do so.

We understand that we should not lapse into a false into a false sense of security that the process will protect each of us.

We understand that while our collaborative attorneys share a commitment to the process described in this document, each of them has a professional duty to represent his or her own client diligently, and is not the attorney for the other party.

IV. ATTORNEY'S FEES AND COSTS

We agree that our attorneys are entitled to be paid for their services, and the first task in a collaborative matter is to ensure parity of payment to each of them. We agree to make funds available for this purpose.

V. PARTICIPATION WITH INTEGRITY

We will work to protect the privacy, respect and dignity of all involved, including parties, attorneys and consultants.

We shall maintain a high standard of integrity and specifically shall not take advantage of each other or of the miscalculations or inadvertent mistakes of others, but shall identify and correct them.

VI. EXPERTS AND CONSULTANTS

If experts are needed, we will retain them jointly unless all parties and their attorneys agree otherwise in writing.

VII. CHILDREN'S ISSUES

In resolving issues about sharing the enjoyment of and responsibility for our children, the parties, attorneys and therapists shall make every effort to reach amicable solutions that promote the children's best interests.

We agree to act quickly to mediate and resolve differences related to the children to promote a caring, loving and involved relationship between the children and both parents.

We agree to insulate our children from involvement in our disputes.

VIII. NEGOITATION IN GOOD FAITH

We acknowledge that each of our attorneys is independent from the other attorneys in the Collaborative Law group, represents only one party in our collaborative marital dissolution process.

We understand that the process, even with full and honest disclosure, will involve vigorous good faith negotiations.

Each of us will be expected to take a reasoned position in all disputes. Where such positions differ, each of us will be encouraged to use our best efforts to create proposals that meet the fundamental needs of both of us and if necessary to compromise to reach a settlement of all issues. Although each of us may discuss the likely outcome of a litigated result, none of us will use threats of litigation as a way of forcing settlement.

IX. ABUSE OF THE COLLABORATIVE PROCESS

We understand that our Collaborative Law attorney will withdraw from a case as soon as possible upon learning that his or her client has withheld or misrepresented information or otherwise acted so as to undermine or take unfair advantage of the Collaborative Law process. Examples of such violations of the process are: the secret disposition of community, quasi-community or separate property, failing to disclose the existence or the collaborative process, abusing the minor children of the parties, or planning to flee the jurisdiction of the court with the children.

X. DISQUALIFICATION BY COURT INTERVENTION

We understand that our attorney' representation is limited to the Collaborative Law process and that neither of our attorneys nor their firms can ever represent us in an adversarial court proceeding against the other spouse regarding their parental or marital rights. Our attorneys can, however, file an action for the entry of a Consent Order or an action for a simple divorce.

In the event we are unable to resolve the issues between ourselves, we agree we shall use _____ as a Mediator to assist us in resolving the issues.

In the event we are not successful at resolving any issue(s) in mediation, we may discuss arbitration or either party may opt out of the collaborative agreement.

In the event a court filing is unavoidable, both attorneys will be disqualified as witnesses and their work product will be inadmissible as evidence unless the parties agree otherwise in writing.

XI. PLEDGE
BOTH PARTIES AND ATTORNEYS HEREBY TO COMPLY WITH AND TO PROMOTE THE SPIRIT AND WRITTEN WORD OF THIS DOCUMENT.

Dated   Dated

_____   _____
Wife signature   Husband signature

_____   _____
Attorney for Wife   Attorney for Husband

APPENDIX C
Checklists and Worksheets

The following worksheets and checklists can be found and downloaded at no cost at learning.institutedfa.com – From the menu bar click on tab – For the Public – U.S. Resources.

- GETTING ORGANIZED
- MY PRIORITIES
- LISTING OF ASSETS
- HOUSEHOLD INVENTORY
- EXPENSE WORKSHEET - All expense items should be documented from amounts paid over the last 12 months from your bank statements and/or credit cards. Using a 12-month cycle accounts for seasonal activity and varying expenses. Be sure to only include expenses for yourself and not your children. If there are any items that you are not sure of, provide an estimated amount and what information you used to determine those amounts. For example, print outs of rental prices in your area or places you may choose to live. An expense worksheet can be used for each credit card and bank account then totaled together to clearly represent your annual expenses.
- GENERIC FINANCIAL AFFIDAVIT – Be prepared to show documentation of each line item if asked. This will eliminate

hours of discussion and save time arguing over expenses. The Expense worksheet above along with a recent pay stub will assist in preparation of your affidavit.

- CHECKLIST TO HELP YOU EVALUATE YOUR SEPARATION AGREEMENT

Having this information prepared prior to
meeting with your attorney and/or CDFA
will save you time and money.

In addition, there are informative articles and a directory
to locate CDFA professionals in your area.

APPENDIX D
Budget for Additional Children's Expenses

These are expenses not generally covered by child support but are important to your family's situation. These items should be addressed in your divorce agreement.

	MONTHLY EXPENSES	EXPLANATION
ADDITIONAL CHILD-RELATED EXPENSES		
Education/Tuition – Private School	$1,527	tuition per invoice
College Expenses	$2,700	estimated
Tutoring/prep classes	$ 150	estimated
Cell phones	$ 200	per invoice
Sport registration fees and equipment	$ 500	YMCA membership, Tennis and Field Hockey
Medical Expenses-not covered by ins.	$	estimated

Dentist/Orthodontist-not covered by ins.	$	estimated
Optometrist/Glasses/ Contacts-not covered by ins.	$	estimated
Car Payment	$	estimated
Car maintenance/ins./ repairs/property taxes	$	estimated
Gas for vehicles	$	estimated
TOTAL CHILD-RELATED EXPENSES	$	Determine how these Expenses will be shared

Sometimes these costs are shared by a percentage split (Mother30%/ Father70%) and some of these expenses are estimated and agreed to when the agreement is signed.

APPENDIX E
Alimony "What If" Scenario

<u>**This is an example of data that can be used for the negotiation process of determining alimony in states where there is no formal calculation.**</u>

Results (Monthly)	Wife	Husband
1. Income After Taxes...	$4850	$4880
. % of Combined Income After Taxes...	50	50

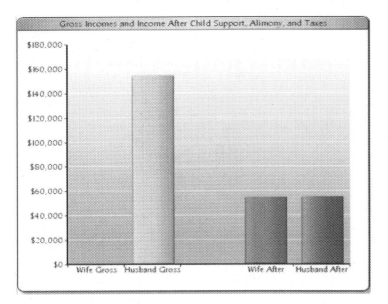

Many individuals prepare budgets that are completely unrealistic and don't even match the amount of income available even when funds are split 50/50 after taxes and child support payments. Providing this information allows each party to manage their expectations. Your lawyer can provide further guidance based on their experience in negotiating alimony.